Stones of

...Without Walls...

By R. Gordon Cashwell

Eagle & Otter Publishing Co.

inside every fat book is a thin book trying to get out

Unless otherwise noted, Scripture Quotations are taken from the New American Standard Bible, Copyright 1960, 1962, 1963, 1968, 1971, 1972, 1973, 1975, 1977, 1995 by the Lockman Foundation (www.lockman.com)

Bible quotations identified KJV are from the King James Version of the Bible.

Cover concept by w. c. hughes
Cover art by Kina Forney – http://www.kina-ink.com

Contact: Gordon Cashwell
         Without Walls Ministry
         P.O. Box 21090
         Charleston, S.C. 29413

Contact: Eagle and Otter Publishing Co. (843-813-5802)

Contents

Introduction

This book began a few years ago as I would relate to people some of the things God was doing in our ministry (Without Walls Ministry). People kept saying, "You need to write that down" or "Are you keeping a record of all of these things?" It turned out that I had been writing things down; keeping a log of answered prayer and encouragements in my prayer journal. Lately, it has seemed that everywhere I have been, people were talking about writing books. God began to speak to me about writing 'for the next generation.'

The title, *Stones of Remembrance...,* comes from the book of Joshua. When the people miraculously crossed the Jordan River on dry ground, Joshua instructed them to take twelve stones and stack them as an altar to remind the future generations about the faithfulness of God. That is what this book is.

This book is not meant to be a theology book, or a book about ministry methods. It is simply a true story of how I found myself having the opportunity of leading an uncommon ministry in an uncommon place. My hope is that its greatest impact will be one of encouragement that God can surely do anything and make something out of nothing.

I have never written a book before, so I spent a lot of time in prayer about this one. As I prayed about the book, I felt God wanted me to tell a story, a kind of testimony. I also had two dreams that were supposed to be a sort of letter for the generation to come. I believe it is a testimony with a message. The story has culminated in the development of a philosophy of ministry that will challenge the status quo. It is a part of what I believe God is speaking to many in the church right now about the future church. It is about what the church will look like as we approach the end. *The first reformation was one of creeds. The coming reformation is one of deeds.* When confronted with the fact that he wanted to bring the church back 50 years, Billy Graham responded, "I do not want to bring it back 50 years. I want to bring it back 2,000 years." May this happen, Lord!

The first part of the book is a series of testimonies showing the grace and power of God that is ours through Jesus Christ, particularly when we reach out to the poor and hurting and engage in winning lost souls and meeting the needs of the poor in a united kingdom fashion. These are the stories that led up to the formation of Without Walls Ministry and helped define it. The last part of the book spells out a vision from God that I believe will happen one day. It is the vision of a church without a building that encompasses many denominations and that focuses on seeking and saving the lost. The church in America today has great potential! If the spiritual, financial and human potential were focused as the Spirit leads, there is no limit to what God can do!

CHAPTER 1

A FIRM FOUNDATION

As stated in the introduction, this book shares the story of the development of a ministry that started with only my family of three. It has culminated in the development of not only a church, Hope Assembly, and a men's house, but also an interdenominational group called Without Walls Ministry. 'Without Walls' tears down walls between churches by uniting them to go outside the walls of the church to minister on the streets of impoverished neighborhoods.

Not only have I not written a book before, but ending up in the ministry was an interesting road for me and was certainly not what I had anticipated. I grew up in a traditional church that was more of a social club than a church. I had never heard the gospel until I was 14 years old at a camp. I went forward to the altar to 'receive Christ', and then struggled with my faith for years--- not really surrendered---and not really understanding Christ's love and what it meant to be a Christian. I was involved in religious activities on and off until I was 22 years old when I met the Savior and began a loving, trusting relationship.

As a result of growing up in a family where alcoholism and addiction was a factor, there was a root of bitterness that had grown inside me. It seemed that no matter how hard I tried, the approval did not come. Like all families, we had problems in our home life. I was pushed to work perfectly in music, my grades, and anything that involved performance for others. Now that I look back, a spirit of rejection, guilt and inferiority had been passed down through generations and left me wanting to prove myself. The bitterness from the alcoholism and the lack of self-esteem from the conditional acceptance manifested itself in depression, insomnia, suicidal thoughts, and a low self-image that pushed me to self-destruction on one side, and to try to prove that I was worth something on the other.

I did not understand myself and why I suffered with these problems. In undergraduate school I attended some Christian activities, but also kept part of my life in the world. I did not understand surrender and the Christian walk and was very frustrated. I was attending church meetings and trying to earn some points with God. I felt God was always there, but never happy with me, always pushing me, and frustrated with me. Although I was the top biology and chemistry student out of over 300 biology and chemistry students at SUNY Albany for more than one semester, I never felt I was worth anything.

As one of the top 5% of medical college applicants, I was accepted into a medical school in Syracuse, N.Y. I was not attending church at the time. The partying I was doing at school and in the Air Force (I had a scholarship) was taking its toll on me. The worse I did in school, the worse I felt about myself. The symptoms of the bitterness and low self-image began to manifest themselves in more insomnia, depression, suicidal thoughts, and even a little 'cutting' of myself. I was not attending church or even seeking to follow God at the time.

As my self-acceptance began to deteriorate due to my

lack of self-esteem, my life became unmanageable and I knew I needed help. This was when I first really understood that God loved me and wanted to help me. Until then, serving God had been a burden, as I was steadily trying to please or win points with Him. I reached out to Him when I needed to and found that as I surrendered, He was there to lovingly catch me. When I knelt beside my bed at medical school and let Jesus in and gave Him control of my life, I felt a peace, warmth and love that I had never felt before.

Immediately, I began to understand His immense love for me, which was something I had not understood before. I started to understand that He loved me, not based on my performance, but based on His grace. I began to feel valuable apart from anything I could do.

As I began to understand His love and pursue Him, it became apparent that there was a problem in my heart. I cried a lot during church services for the first few weeks as a Christian. It was as if God was massaging my heart. This was new to me. Being an adult child of an alcoholic, I had learned to 'stuff' my feelings and deny them, but now they were all coming to the surface as I trusted God. Along with the brokenness came the bitterness and anger I did not even know were there. I had to learn to forgive those who had hurt me. I started with the alcoholics in the family and went from there. As I forgave, which was a process, my life became much happier, stronger and stable. I also began to weep over those whom I myself had hurt. I found ways to convey my remorse to them and ask them to forgive me and try to make it up to them.

One of the first things I learned was that I was worth something no matter what people thought about me or my performance. That was a new concept to me-

--unconditional love! At the first church I attended as a surrendered Christian, which was a Baptist church, the pastor gave me two Scriptures because he knew I was struggling with my self-perception. One was Psalms 139:13–14, "For Thou didst form my innermost parts; Thou didst weave me in my mother's womb. I will praise Thee, for I am fearfully and wonderfully made...Wonderful are Thy works, and my soul knows it very well." The other was Galatians 2:20, "I have been crucified with Christ, and it is no longer I who live, but Christ lives in me; and the life which I now live in the flesh I live by faith in the Son of God, who loved me, and delivered Himself up for me."

It was then that I began to learn the power and importance of Scripture memory. I found that I was truly transformed by the renewing of my mind. (Romans 12:2). I began to understand that I was saved by grace through faith. (Ephesians 2:8) That was the mustard seed of faith that grew the more I fed it with the Word. I memorized many of the promises of God, for faith comes by hearing, and hearing by the Word of God. (Romans 10:17)

About a month after my salvation experience, my brother invited me to a conference called BASIC--- "Brothers and Sisters in Christ." At this conference I first heard about the Holy Spirit and the need to be filled with the Holy Spirit. They laid hands on me and prayed and I immediately began speaking in tongues. What a wonderful experience with the Holy Spirit! I know we have differing opinions of what it means to be filled with the Spirit, but we can all agree that we need Him! I have been exposed to many different facets of orthodox Christianity that have differing beliefs on the baptism or filling of the Holy Spirit. I feel we can agree on some things. We will not be fruitful without the Spirit's filling, and one of the by-products of the Spirit's filling is saved souls. Jesus said we would receive power to be His witnesses through the filling of the Spirit (Acts 1:8). I always tell people who want to debate me on the Spirit's baptism that whatever they believe, I want to see proof that their opinion is right. The proof that I look for is souls truly being saved, discipled, trained, filled and sent out to save more souls. If this is not happening, in my humble opinion, the proof is not there. I suggest we look at the stats and find out who is really succeeding at this and join them. Life is too short and the end-times are rolling in too fast for us to miss out. This is serious business!

The worship leader at the BASIC retreat was from Syracuse where I was living and he invited me to his church. I went and it was the most amazing church I had ever been in. I had not heard much modern music in a church and had never sung 'off the wall'. All the churches I had been in previously had either song-sheets or hymn books. When the pastor spoke, I felt as though he was speaking directly to me.

I also began to hear the Holy Spirit speak to me for the first time. Once, I was in class at medical school and our Jewish professor mentioned that he had a lung infection and asked if any of the medical students had a cure for it. God spoke to me and said, "Go and pray for him." I was not sure if it was God, but on the way back from church that Sunday a girl from our class said, "Our Jewish professor asked the other day if anyone had a cure for his lungs. I knew God spoke to me and said to go and pray for him, so I went to the front of the class and asked if I could pray for him. He let me pray---and he was healed!" Wow! She was bold and obedient enough to act when God spoke. I remember feeling the regret that I had missed out on a great opportunity and committing not to miss one again.

The next time I heard the Holy Spirit was in an elevator. God told me to stop a man who was leaving the elevator and tell him that the Bible says, "A righteous man falls seven times but rises again." I told him. He stopped and held the elevator door and said, "You know, I used to be into that Christian stuff. I have backslid and my girlfriend and I were high last night. We were dancing in the street and she was hit by a car and the doctors are not sure she is going to make it." When I heard him say that, the Spirit came over me and I said, "I am going to pray for her and she will get better." I saw him a few days later and he confirmed that she got better!

Another time I heard God was in the weight room while working out. God told me to tell a man that his Mom was praying for him. He was very popular and had many girlfriends. He was a partier and was not showing any interest in God. One day in the weight room, before I said anything directly to him, I said out loud, "Praise the Lord!" He said, "My mom is always saying that." I thought to myself, "Wow! This is for real." I was almost scared by it. Again, I decided I did not want to miss any other opportunities.

During this time I was really struggling in school. I was not sure I wanted to stay enrolled and it seemed God was confirming to stay, but I did not want to. I was struggling with a fear of failure, a fear of success, a desire to escape, a passion for Jesus and ministry, and an attempt to discern how to follow the Spirit's leading. One day I was at the church and I said to God, "God, I feel you are calling me to leave medical school and go into ministry. If that is true I need You to make it very clear." I was really wrestling at this point with a fear of failure and at the same time, a passion for God. The pastor stopped preaching and said, "I know there is someone here who thinks being a doctor is a high calling, but God is calling you to a higher calling which is ministry." I thought, "That may have been a coincidence." At another church service, I asked God, "God, if you are leading me to leave and go to Bible school, what am I going to tell my parents?" From the pulpit, the pastor said, "Don't worry about what you are going to tell your parents. Just trust God and go to Bible school. They will understand some day." I was still not convinced. At another service, I thought, "Hmm, this is working pretty well. I will ask another question. God, how will I pay for Bible school?" The pastor stopped preaching and said, "Don't worry about paying for Bible school. God will provide. Just go and trust Him."

Well, I still struggled. Because of the emotional turmoil I was going through during my first semester in medical school, I had failed a couple classes. I tried to make them up during the summer, but was not able. My own failure had brought me to a turning point. I had to either repeat my first year of medical school or go to Bible school. God was very gracious to me. I ended up leaving and going to Columbia Biblical Seminary in Columbia, SC. This was the school my pastor went to, and as I prayed I felt the Lord leading me there. This school is now called Columbia International University.

Seminary was interesting. I learned a lot about church history, theology and the philosophy of ministry. I mostly learned how to grow in Christ. I also learned that even though there are many different facets of Christianity, we have a common bond in Christ. At first, I did not understand that God worked in many ways through many different expressions of the same faith. Having grown up in a mainline church that sang from outdated hymn books, when we went to chapel and had to sing out of hymn books, I questioned it. I thought that since the vibrant faith I found was expressed through modern songs sung 'off the wall', God could not be in the old hymns. At the mainline church I attended growing up, some of the people did not accept that the Bible was the Word of God. Many of them were very involved in the world and the church was a kind of social club. I do not remember any witnessing or evangelistic sermons. I connected hymn-singing with this false religious spirit and I did not believe God could use such an old worn-out method. At college, however, I heard the people sing the hymns with gusto and sincerity. I became acquainted with many of the Christians who liked these hymns and discovered they had a faith that, in many cases, went deeper than mine. God challenged me to see each group of believers as vital expressions of His kingdom.

It was in seminary that I really began to learn to trust God for provision. My parents' church wanted to send me monthly money, but since they were of a denomination that was striving for world peace and healthy ecology while neglecting the gospel and not teaching that the Bible was clearly the Word of God, I would not accept the money. I felt that God did not want me to be unequally yoked. I finished my first semester and was totally out of money. I had no idea what I was going to do.

I had $300 in a bank account, and as I prayed I thought about tithing. My parents had given me $3,000 and I had not tithed on it. I spoke to our dorm director and some friends, and they all said the same thing. I had to give my last money to the church. Well, on a Sunday I gave it. The next day I called my pastor in New York. He said, "Pray for me, Gordon. Yesterday (that Sunday), I felt so strongly that you needed money that I sent you

$1,500. I did not ask the board, but I sent it anyway." I was amazed. What kind of God is this?

At the end of my first year in Bible school, I began to feel regret about leaving medical school. I would be up at night crying, sensing I had let my father down. He had paid for my undergraduate education and had even paid off debts for me that I owed from medical school. When I went to visit a friend in New York who discipled me, he told me that God had been speaking to him about me. He said, "I feel you have been up at night crying with regrets and feeling you have let your father down. I feel God wants you to know that he is proud of you for the decision you have made and that you need to stick with it." I thanked my friend and praised God for His wonderful direction!

My philosophy of ministry began to develop in seminary. First of all, we were taught to let the Bible speak for itself and then ask the Holy Spirit to show us how to apply the intended meaning of the author to our lives. As I studied, I noticed some predominant themes, particularly in the teachings of Jesus. As I looked at my life and compared it with what I read, I did not like what I saw.

One teaching was *evangelism and discipleship---the Great Commission.* Not just to have an evangelism program in the church, but to have a ministry that was effectively truly saving lost souls and then seeing them healed and equipped to be sent out into the harvest fields. Because of the wonderful healing I had experienced in my life, I had a hunger for souls that motivated me to be involved in evangelism. I tried the programs in the church and through them learned the mechanics of actually sharing the gospel, but I did not observe anyone who was truly a new convert that was actually saved and discipled and equipped for ministry through these programs. It seemed as if no one was interested in making converts. Sure, the church I was in was growing, but often at the expense of other churches as people transferred from their church to our church. Admittedly, the evangelism program I was in was structured more to train people how to share the gospel rather than on producing the fruit of the gospel.

Interestingly, even though some of the churches I was familiar with were 'growing', the church in America, in general, was not. For example, in the 1990s, not one county in the continental United States reported an increase in church attendance. Church attendance in the 90s fell by 19.4%. That meant that even though some of the churches were 'growing', it had to be mostly through 'transfer' growth. As a matter of fact, only 1% of 'evangelical' churches in the United States are actually winning and discipling lost people. I thought God made us fishers of men, not swappers of fish from one aquarium to the other. As I was observing objectively, it seemed that souls were not being won. In addition to this, it is important to note that North America is the only continent in the world where Christianity is not growing. The United States has the fourth largest population of unchurched people in the world, after China, India and Malaysia.[1] Churches currently lose 2,765,000 people per year in America. Something must be wrong with the American church if we are losing ground so rapidly.

Another teaching I received as I 'let the Bible speak for itself' was that of the importance of *ministry to the poor*. Throughout the Bible, an outworking and even proof of someone's walk with God was interest in relieving the needs of the poor. Whether it was a call in Leviticus to leave gleanings for the poor, a Psalm of David stating that

God would reward those who help the poor (Psalm 41), a proverb of Solomon equating helping the poor with lending to God, a call from Isaiah to help the poor as part of true fasting and worship (Isaiah 58), or a call from Jesus to sell all and give to the poor as a proof of faith, I could not ignore this call. James 2:14-17 says, "What use is it, my brethren, if someone says he has faith but he has no works? Can that faith save him? If a brother or sister is without clothing and in need of daily food, and one of you says to them, 'Go in peace, be warmed and be filled,' and yet do not give them what is necessary for their body, what use is that? Even so faith, if it has no works, is dead, being by itself." God equates the outworking of our faith with the work of relieving the needs of the poor.

Now I knew that the churches I was involved in were giving to different 'ministries' that served the poor, and that was great. However, the majority of these 'ministries' were not preaching good news to the poor, binding up the brokenhearted, and setting the captives free. (Isaiah 61, Luke 4:18-19). They were meeting some physical needs, but were not open about faith in Jesus Christ. Also, I did not understand why we did not have any poor people in our churches. Out of hundreds of people that attended, I did not know one homeless person or one person who lived in public housing. As a matter of fact, I did not even know one poor person myself. I began to feel God challenging me that I was missing out on an important aspect of my walk with God.

In our missions classes, as we studied the different countries, I also noticed that the places where there seemed to be the most fruitful evangelism happening were in areas of poverty. As James said, "Listen, my dear brothers: Has not God chosen those who are poor in the eyes of the world to be rich in faith and to inherit the kingdom He promised to those who love Him?" People in physical need recognize their spiritual need more readily. These souls are just as important as those who have more riches.

Another teaching was the importance of *church planting*. According to statistics, church planting is the most effective way of true soul-winning. As a matter of fact, younger churches are much more effective per capita at winning souls, which means new converts and not just transfer from one church to another. In addition, smaller churches are much more effective per capita at winning souls than are larger ones. The larger the church the greater the cost and the greater the number of Christians it takes to win a new convert. As a matter of fact, it has been proven that new churches and groups bring new people.

As I pondered these things, I began to ask God to send me to a place where there were many people in physical and spiritual need so I could plant churches and have a maximized harvest. I lived in Columbia, S.C., and while finishing seminary began to ask God what I should do. I really expected to be able to go overseas and plant churches where there is a great harvest. For whatever reason, God did not allow that.

As I asked Him to use me, I realized there was a mission field right in my back yard. Columbia, S.C. is one of the largest cities in S.C., but, at that time, there was only one Assemblies of God church within the city limits (downtown) and it was a 'house' church. I began to ask God about establishing a church in downtown Columbia. As I asked God and began to make plans, other people began to be interested in establishing a downtown Assemblies of God church. Mike Oney, a home missionary, had a vision for it. We talked together about it. God spoke to me that I was not ready to establish a church but that I should join with him. Another man named Ned Crosby joined in. He became the senior pastor and I became a home missionary so I could help him with the evangelism and setting up the infrastructure of the church. We became Capital City Church.

The cooperation in the Columbia Assemblies of God churches helped us and we started with a strong core group. With the Lord's help, a small group began to meet in 1993. We reached out together to the neighborhoods downtown and saw fruit. I went and spoke on weekends and met with people in order to raise my budget to support my family.

HEALINGS

While at Capital City Church, I began to learn more about the power of prayer. I learned that God could do anything. He began to show Himself strong in miracles, signs and wonders. One way was healings. Our daughter, Kara, was born with an intestinal blockage. She had to have surgery on her first day. The doctors gave her an ileostomy. This is one of those bags attached to her side she used instead of her diaper. The doctors did not know the cause for the blockage. At three months of age, they diagnosed her with cystic fibrosis.

The doctors explained that cystic fibrosis (cf) is a genetic disease. It had no cure and was fatal. According to them she would have trouble gaining weight. She would have to have respiratory therapy three times a day. She would have lung infections and be in the hospital a lot. Her lungs would deteriorate and eventually she would die.

They could reverse the ileostomy surgery, but not the cf.

My wife, Kim, and I were devastated. We prayed. I cried a lot and asked God for strength. As was expected, Kara could not digest her food well. Even with enzymes, she had trouble with food. She was not gaining weight like she should. We gave her respiratory therapy three times a day. Lung infections sent her to the hospital more than once her first year. I just knew we were in for a long fight.

When Kara was one year old, Kim took her to a healing service. When they came home that night, Kim was beaming. She claimed that Kara had been healed. I wanted to believe it but I was really concerned about Kim. I wondered why those people had raised her hopes so high. I told Kim that maybe we just needed to have faith to make it through the trials. I did not want her to be disappointed.

Interestingly enough, the coughing went away. The lung infections stopped. She gained weight. We slowly inched her off the respiratory therapy. Soon, all we were giving her was her enzymes. I could not believe it, but it appeared as though she was healed! Praise God.

As I write, Kara is 14 years old and doing great. She has not been in the hospital for another lung infection since that healing service. She is one of the tallest in her class and plays softball and volleyball. We do not give her therapy often. The doctors are amazed. Actually, I am amazed! What a wonderful Savior we serve! Praise God!

A man from Beaufort, S.C. had heard me speak at his church. When his niece had an aneurism in Columbia, he called me to see if I would go to the hospital and pray for her. I called Pastor Ned and we went together. When we arrived at the ICU, the nurse informed us that we were not allowed in her room. She was to be kept in total isolation with no sound and no light before her brain surgery. God had spoke to me that I needed to actually lay hands on her, not just pray from a distance, so I told the nurse that I strongly felt that I needed to be in the room. He asked the girl's mother, "Does she believe in this?" The mother began to cry and hesitated for a moment because they did not attend church, and through her tears, managed to squeeze out a very weak "Yes." The nurse let us in and Pastor Ned and I laid hands on her and prayed. Because of the damage done to her brain, she could not speak and did not seem to recognize even her mother. The room was pitch black and we could barely see her but God gave me a confidence deep inside that something was happening in the realm of faith.

The doctor informed us there was a 50% chance that she would make it through the surgery but that there was only a 10% chance she would ever walk or talk again and that she would never do anything such as drive a car again. The hours in the surgery waiting area were intense. You could feel the tension and apprehension in the room and hear the family crying. When the doctor came out, we all held our breath and then he announced that she had made it through the surgery. There was a great cheering and many tears. I gathered the family together and we prayed and rejoiced. She eventually made a full recovery---walking, driving, speaking, reading, and writing---and she became a part of our church!

As our days in Columbia went on, we saw God transform lives. We saw Him provide in miraculous ways and a closely knit congregation was established. In 1996, God began to move on my heart to go to Charleston, S.C. and plant a church. Charleston was another city that did not have an Assemblies of God church within the city limits. I was concerned that my wife may not want to go since all her family lived in Columbia. I prayed. One day I brought the idea before Kim. I was surprised when she agreed with me that we should move to Charleston to establish a church. We began to ask the Holy Spirit how He wanted us to begin. As usual, He guided us clearly.

CHAPTER 2

CHARLESTON: SOMETHING FROM NOTHING

We began to make plans. I started travelling to Charleston and familiarizing myself with the city. There was one hitch. Because Kara had been diagnosed with cystic fibrosis, no insurance company wanted to insure us. At that time, Kim was working as a phlebotomist. She was working for a lab company and she had insurance through them, but they did not have any phlebotomy openings in Charleston. As we made our plans, we decided that God wanted us to move in the summer of 1997. Kim and I agreed that we should just move and expect God to provide.

Two weeks before we moved, Kim's boss called her in the office and said that their company was opening phlebotomy positions in Charleston and wanted to know if Kim would work at one of them. Praise God! God was already going before us!

The first few years in Charleston were very difficult. Because of the history of the city and the history of 'inner-city' work there, there was a great distrust of myself and the work in the neighborhood of our church location. It seemed we were constantly being tested. One way was through theft. Every few months, someone broke the windows in front of the church to steal something. We had a security system, but by the time I or the police arrived (whoever was first---I beat them often even though I lived six miles away), the culprit was long gone. The police did not seem too interested in detective work on our thefts. They had more important crimes to solve, like the 15 or so shootings that occurred each year within ten blocks of the church. I remember the lonely feeling of boarding up the windows of the church by myself in the middle of the night after someone broke in. I spent the first few years scared much of the time.

I continually asked God why I was there and how He was going to make a church out of just me and my family. One day He replied by saying, "I made the universe out of nothing. I can make a church out of nothing, thank you very much!" I began to trust Him and not give up.

We were tested through threats as well. The first few years I was there, my life was threatened at least five times. One man pulled a knife on me. He also threatened to gather a group of people from the neighborhood with guns and clubs and burn the church down. Another man pointed a gun at me in the housing projects. I could see the laser pointing at my head. One young man punched me and cracked my tooth. Others just simply assured me that they were going to get rid of me. Sometimes it was hard to keep going. At times my wife would want to leave. One night after I was threatened, we were lying in bed. My wife thought I was asleep and I could hear her crying, saying she wanted to go home. This broke my heart. I comforted her asking her not to be afraid and reminded her how God had been with us. Then I said, "Kim, we cannot leave now. We have raised some people's hopes."

Circumstances such as these, when coupled with the constant financial needs and the lack of workers, caused me to want to quit. Every month or so I would go to God and say, "Am I in the right place? I do not want to be doing anything You are not a part of." He would always reassure me. One time I took a group from the church to the revival at Brownsville, Florida. I was so discouraged that I told the Lord that if He did not speak clearly to me, I was going to quit this ministry. A man whom I was discipling had been off the streets for a while and had stayed off drugs and alcohol, but was constantly with the wrong crowd. I kept warning him, telling him that as a Christian he should not be close friends and companions with nonbelievers, especially those who were drinking and doing drugs since he was trying to stop. We talked about it often, even in the van on the way to Brownsville.

When Steve Hill (at Brownsville Assembly of God) began to preach, he kept addressing the issue of not being unequally yoked and not hanging around with people who drank and used drugs if you used to be on the streets and doing these things but now were saved and trying to stop. I leaned over and elbowed my new friend and said, "He's talking to you, you know." He just laughed. Then an interesting thing happened. Steve Hill began to say that the people who were helping those off the streets and working in the inner-city were real heroes and that he knew they wanted to quit but not to quit even though it was hard. He went on and on, and even though my friend did not know what I was going through, he snickered and leaned over and said, "And now he is talking to you!" Thank You Jesus! You knew I needed that!

After we persevered for a while, I began to realize some of the initial trials were just tests. I do not think anyone really meant me any harm. They may have just wanted to see where I was coming from. As a matter of fact, I feel very safe and welcome in the inner-city now. People who go door-to-door with us for the first time are usually amazed at how receptive and friendly the people are.

Some workers think they cannot be effective because they are not 'tough' enough or cannot relate to the culture because they are not from an inner-city background. Actually, what I am finding is that *neighborhoods with crime, unrest, disorder and poverty are looking for a different spirit to come in. They are looking for kindness, gentleness and order.*

I began to see the favor of God in many ways. One time I went down the street to Food Lion. They had opened just before our church had opened, so I figured we had something in common. I went down and asked them if we could hand out flyers in their parking lot. The lady was not a manager and did not officially represent Food Lion. She said to me, "What color church is it." I knew what she meant since this grocery store was meant to provide jobs for the community which was mostly African-American. I went back to the church feeling rejected.

Not long after that, I wrote on my prayer list that I needed favor from Food Lion. A few weeks later as I was praying about this, we had a baptism service at Faith Assembly of God in Summerville. After the service, my wife was excitedly talking to a lady. She introduced her as a girl she grew up with at South Congaree Assembly (Columbia, S.C.). She introduced me to her husband. He began to testify to me that he had just gotten saved the month before. He said that a vending machine fell on him at his business and broke his back. He told God that if He healed him he would give his life to God. God did heal his back and he surrendered. As we were talking, he realized where our church was. He said, "You know what? I am the head manager at a Food Lion down the street from yours. Let me know if you need anything and we will help you." I was overjoyed and let him know

I had been praying for favor with that very Food Lion!

This began our relationship with Food Lion that still exists today. Each year for the past several years, we have been picking up groceries from Food Lions around the area. They have also donated $5,000 to the Convoy of Hope (an outreach party we host each year for a national organization) for the past few years and their vendors have given us thousands of pounds of groceries for that outreach yearly. Isn't it amazing? It all started with a little prayer for favor from Food Lion!

It has been fun to watch this relationship with Food Lion progress. In 2009, we were concerned for the Convoy of Hope because the lady who helped make the decisions for the grants we applied for from Food Lion, who was on the management team for Convoy, had moved to another job for another company. The previous year, the people who make decisions on grants for Food Lion asked someone whom she had worked with in the past what they should do about the grant. She said "yes". This year, they were asking the regional manager. The Food Lion grants department was concerned that they were not receiving enough return on the investment with Convoy. They had a new regional manager that had just been hired. When they asked for her advice on the grant, she said, "I love Convoy of Hope! My husband has coordinated the electricity for it for years!" I did not know it, but her husband had been on our management team for a long time! Go God! You went before us!

Another struggle was the building situation in downtown Charleston. We were very blessed to pay about 10 cents per square foot per month for rent from the very beginning. The going rate at that time was $1.20 per square foot! God had shown me this building and I did not realize there had been four other ministries in the building before we came. Apparently, the owners were Christians and were praying that the building would be devoted for His work. God had simply drawn me to the building.

In the process of time we expanded and began to use different parts of the building. We remodeled a room for clothing distribution, one for King's Kidz, one for food storage, a utility room, tool room and more. After about six years in the building, we began to plan for our men's house. We finally realized that we had a whole upstairs floor that was not being used. It took us a couple of years, but we reframed all the downstairs ceilings (about 7,000 square feet) and hung two layers of fire-rated sheetrock. Then we put in an emergency stairwell and began the upstairs 4,000 square feet. We took a big empty space and built walls, a bathroom, a kitchen, dorm rooms, and more. We had to run all of the electricity, heating and air, plumbing, flooring, and ceilings. We were excited to see it finished.

But then a major test of our faith happened. When we were almost finished and ready to let men in to the facility, a family member of the owner of the building asked me out to lunch. He said that he, sadly, had to let me know, even though we had put so much work into the building, that they were selling it and that it was going to be torn down to make condominiums. We had about a year left in the building. At first I was devastated. How could God have let us put so much time, money and effort into this building and then not allow us to use it?

Well, I began to pray and God began to speak to me. He let me know that we did not need to move, but to just sit still. I did not know what He had planned, but the message was clear. The first people to panic were those who sold the buildings. They were Christians and friends of mine and they insisted on helping us find another place to move. I simply let them know that it was not God's plan for us to move. They did not know what to do. I did not know what to do either. It was hard to know what God was up to. I did not know whether we would have a building or not. I thought maybe God might have us meet on the street but I was trusting Him.

The next people to panic were our neighbors. They too had been bought out and knew that by the next October the buildings would be torn down. The chiropractor from next door asked what we were going to do. I told him, "nothing". I let him know that the Lord had told us not to do anything. He said, "Okay. Then I will not move either." That lasted for a few months until one day he came over and said that he was going to move. Apparently, he knew someone in the development company that bought the buildings. They had 'inside information' that confirmed our fears. He moved to another location around the corner.

Then a developer friend of mine became greatly concerned. He took me out to lunch the same day the chiropractor spoke to me. He was very concerned because he knew the new owners. He wanted to help us find a place. I told him not to worry. We did not need to move.

I think all of these people thought I was crazy. Little did they know what was about to happen. The next month, the local newspaper that owned the property around ours called me. They said, "We just bought your buildings and we want you to stay." Wow! Another miracle! My developer friend took me out to lunch again. He said, "You have my attention now. Things like that do not just happen." He began bringing a group of people down monthly to feed our church. The chiropractor began offering free therapy at the church weekly-meeting. The previous owner joined in with Without Walls, which is our non-profit ministry that unites churches and organizations in outreach. He coordinates the cooking of food for our large outreaches. People are amazed when God does something!!

The church made more and more progress. As people were saved, discipled, and trained, they entered the ministry with us. It was our philosophy of ministry to raise up leaders from the community where the church was located. This posed some interesting challenges. The first challenge was the distrust that the people in inner-city Charleston felt towards us. I did not understand this at first. Having grown up in upstate New York, I did not understand the racial tensions that had arisen from the history of a southern city like Charleston.

God spoke to me early on to read about the history of Charleston and that understanding it would help me in the ministry here. I believe if anyone is going to make an impact on a city, they need to understand its history. I read a book entitled *Charleston! Charleston!*[2] From this reference, I learned that during colonial times Charleston was considered the capital of the south; thirty percent of all slaves in America were imported into America through Charleston; the ordinances of secession from the Union were signed in Charleston. The Civil War actually started in Charleston as well. The city had more slaves than free people before the Civil War and this caused distrust on the part of the slave owners.

They were so afraid of an uprising that they would not allow the slaves to have their own churches. When

George Whitefield came to Charleston, he was thrown in jail for two weeks for libel and slander against the Anglican Church leaders because he claimed that they should win the poor and the slaves to Christ. He felt they were falling down on their job. Revivalists, like Methodist ministers, were thrown out of town during the Great Awakening. When slave churches started, some of them became prominent. A church led by a man named Morris Brown had an attendance in the thousands. The slave owners became very suspicious, so they framed some of the leaders in the slave community. They hung some, ran the rest out of town, burned the slaves' church buildings down, forced the slaves to worship with them and to sit in the back of the 'white' churches.

Even after the slaves were freed, African-Americans were threatened and intimidated to scare them from voting. After the initial first years of turmoil, the city council was completely white. The first black city councilmember was not elected until the 1960s. Needless to say, after the Civil War, the freed slaves started their own churches and the two races became very separate in their worship. So, here I come into this historical setting as a young white man with a flat top hair cut and an old police car that I bought from an auction asking people to get in the car with me and come to church. Needless to say, people were not rushing head over heels to jump in the car!

Another challenge was the lack of trust due to the history of some of the ministries that had existed to meet the needs of the people. At the time that God showed me the building we should meet in, I did not know four ministries had existed in that building previous to ours. All of them felt as though they needed to be there to meet physical and spiritual needs. All of them ended quickly and tragically. One man's wife left him and he had so many financial problems he had to quit. Another man's wife contracted a strange disease and ended up in a wheelchair. They had financial problems as well and closed the ministry in less than a year. The ministry that was there before ours only lasted seven months before the pastor was divorced, had a heart attack, and then closed down the business.

I believe one of the reasons we were able to survive was that I had 400 people on my prayer chain who I asked specifically to pray for me and would mail out specific prayer requests. I wanted to plant a church in Columbia, S.C., but other people came in with the same vision. My pastor gave me a choice---either join them or start a church myself. God reminded me that it was too difficult for me at that point and that I should join with them on the team. I did. Due to this fact, I was given status as a U.S. missionary with the Assemblies of God and was able to speak at churches and raise finances. It was the very people I was able to contact through this support-raising that became the prayer partners for the future.

We prayed and prayed and reached out and reached out. Slowly, but surely, a little church began to form out of the people in the city that we were reaching. If it were not for the Lord doing the work, nothing would have been done. He showed us over and over that He was with us, not to worry, but to press on.

CHAPTER 3

MANNA FROM HEAVEN

Once again, as we moved forward, we were amazed at the power of God! I could not believe how many times God miraculously provided. I have never seen anything like it. I believe God's heart is so much into reaching out to the poor and brokenhearted that He is willing to meet needs in a powerful way when we design plans with His guidance to touch others.

As we saw God come through miraculously, I began to realize a pattern that is taught in the Word of God. There are Biblical principles in prayer that we inadvertently followed throughout our ministry in Charleston, although we may not have realized we were following them. First of all, many times as we were petitioning, we either wanted something very strongly, or we were seeking God and God guided us, and then we begin to petition Him for what He had promised. Several principles come into play here.

The first principle is that of *crying out*. Psalm 34:6 says, "This poor man cried [literally 'cried out loudly'] and the Lord heard him and saved him out of all his troubles." We see the Bible examples of Hannah crying out for a son, Blind Bartimaeus crying out for healing, Jehosophat crying out for safety (II Chronicles 18:31 and chapter 20), Hezekiah crying out for mercy (Isaiah 38), the psalmists crying out for help, etc. I believe God answers sometimes simply because He hears the cries of His beloved children.

This happened to us at times when we were desperate. One night at Tuesday night prayer we were desperate. We had a team coming to town the next day and we did not have any food to feed them. We also had a back-to-school party that weekend and we needed a couple of thousand dollars. A lady in our church cried out to God in desperation. She took off her shoes and walked around the church and prayed that our empty pantry would be filled until it overflowed. She cried out for the food and $2,000. The next morning, I went to the food bank and all they had was plates and tin foil. While I was purchasing some of the plates and tinfoil, the church called and said the team had arrived. I was discouraged as I walked out to my vehicle crying out to God and wondering how we were going to feed the team.

Surprisingly, after I left the building, a lady who worked there came to find me in the parking lot. She pointed to a semi-truck that was pulling in and said, "Look, Pastor!" Amazingly, the truck was full of all kinds of food! I bought so much food that the pantry was overflowing. On the day of the back-to-school party the team gave us over $2,500. I did not know that they had been collecting money and were planning on giving it to us. I was overwhelmed with joy. Once again, God waited until the last minute and then provided miraculously!

This same lady cried out for her sons who were in the Navy Nuclear school at the Navy Base. When we went to school's graduation, she informed me that she had been praying for the whole class to excel, for all of them to pass and for them to have a record-breaking class. When one of the leaders (Navy Nuclear School) spoke, he said, "We do not know what happened. For the first time everyone passed and we have had a record-breaking class this year!" I chucked as I watched this church member stand up and yell "Hallelujah! Praise God!" in front of all those regimented people.

Another time at all-night prayer we were desperate. We needed $3,000 by that Tuesday. We cried out and cried out that Friday night until early the next morning. We did not receive it until Tuesday. On Tuesday, a boyfriend of one of the ladies at the church came by and said, "My girlfriend told me to give you this. It was right off the top, just like you taught us!" After he left I opened the envelope and it was over two thousand dollars! I still have no idea where it came from. Then a businessman came in and said, "The Lord told me to come by and give you this." It was over a thousand dollars! WOW!

Another principle is that of *praying according to His will.* We see examples of this in Joshua taking the Promised Land, Moses parting the Red Sea, Elijah predicting and praying for rain, and many other incidences. Jesus said, "If you abide in Me and my Words abide in you, ask whatever you wish, and it shall be done for you." (John 15: 7) I John 5:14 –15 says, "And this is the confidence which we have before Him, that, if we ask anything according to His WILL, He hears us. And if we know that He hears us in whatever we ask, we know that we have the requests which we have asked from Him." *Answered prayer often comes in response to us hearing what He wants to do and then seeking Him and asking until we see it come to pass.*

Sometimes, I just did not know what to do. For example, I prayed for years to lose weight and nothing happened. I did not seem to have the self-control to do so. One day I felt God ask me why I wanted to lose weight. I responded that I wanted to look and feel better and be healthier. I realized as God worked on me that there was nothing I could remember in the Bible about it being sinful to be overweight. I did, however, remember that it was wrong to be a glutton. I began to pray about not being a glutton. At this point, my wife entered a program to lose weight. I noticed that not only did she lose weight but her attitude was different. I checked out some of the teaching and it was some of the best Biblical teaching on the bondage of gluttony and how to overcome it. The next semester I enrolled in the class for twelve weeks. This was over five years ago. During the first few months after the class, I lost over 50 pounds and I have kept it off since! When I changed my prayer to praying according to His will, He heard me!

Another principle that we saw God use in prayer is that of *righteous prayer*. None of us is righteous in and of ourselves. It is all by grace that we enter the throne room. However, the Bible clearly states, "If I regard wickedness in my heart, the Lord will not hear." (Psalm 66:18) James 5:16 says that "the effectual fervent prayer of a righteous man availeth much." (KJV) I Peter 3:7 tells us to be careful how we treat our wives so that our prayers are not hindered. Jesus mentioned the importance of us forgiving others before God would forgive us.

An example of righteous prayer came another time when we needed a copier. I called a program that donates money for copiers. I asked for $2,000 and was turned down. I sent out many letters and emails but no one responded. I prayed and a church called me from Columbia that week and asked if we needed a copier. I said, "Did you receive my email?" They said they had not received my email but they had a used copier to give away, and after they prayed God instructed them to give it to me. It was a copier worth $14,000!

One time that copier broke down. A young man who was travelling down from Columbia, S.C. to work with us on the weekends was using it and it broke. I tried and tried to fix it but could not. I prayed and prayed, but to no avail. God began to convict me and let me know why it was broken. The young man had been seeing his girlfriend in Charleston and wanted her to stay with him at the church overnight. I did not let them because it was not right. He decided this particular weekend that he would just stay in a tent at a county park with her. I somehow convinced myself, since we needed help so badly, that it was none of my business since they were not staying at the church. God told me to confront them and that he would fix the copier. We were working late at the church and I went to him about midnight and confronted him. I told him that as much as we needed help, I could not accept help from him if he was living in sin. He left. Immediately, God began to give me instruction on the copier. I opened doors and even slammed things, and then it started right up. God was not going to answer the prayer until I stopped "regarding iniquity."

I did not hear from this young man for a while. Then, one day, I found out that he had left college to pursue ministry. He became a staff member of a church where a friend of mine pastored. He ended up bringing a team down one time to minister with us. Oh, what a blessed redeemer we have! He is planning to bring a team from another church this coming year as well!

Another important principle in prayer is in *not neglecting the poor*. God said in His Word that if we close our ears to the poor, God will close His ears to our prayer. I feel that this is one of the reasons we have had the opportunity to see so many miracles! When I was tested for cancer and when Kara was sick with cystic fibrosis, God gave me

Psalm 41. It states that the man who considers the poor is blessed and that God restores him from his sickbed. Thank God, in both cases he did!

Another principle connected with prayer in the Bible is *sowing and reaping*. God rebuked the people for robbing Him of tithes and offerings in Malachi. He warned them that He would not provide because of that. God said in His Word that if we close our ears to the poor, God would close His ears to our cries (Proverbs 21:13).

Sometimes, the provision seemed to come in response to our own giving. One time we were in need. I felt God had asked me what I would do if He gave our church $10,000. It was so clear that I actually wrote down a list of what I would do with $10,000. In the next three weeks our income seemed to freeze. I asked God what to do and what was happening. He led me on a fast and I began to fast and pray. After a week or so, I was in the living room before church service. At four in the morning, God spoke to me and said, "Give $350 from your church to the Dream Center in Los Angeles." While walking and praying, I found a letter from the Dream Center saying that they needed $180 sponsors for bus seats for their bus ministry. I thought, "That's it. We'll sponsor two seats for $360!" I approached the church and told them that the first $360 from the offering would go to the bus seats.

That afternoon, I went home and a pastor from the Charlotte area had called me. He said he wanted to take me to lunch the next day. When we went to lunch, he gave me $600 that the men from his church had collected. The next day, I received $2,000 from two other churches in the mail. The next day, we received another few thousand. On Wednesday, I received a letter from a lady from First Baptist Church. She said, "In September, you spoke at our church. God touched my heart but I did not have anything to give. I hope this $5,000 helps." Wow! The $10,000 came in---in 3 days!

I have been amazed at how God has blessed us as we have given. Thirteen years as an inner-city ministry and we have increased in income every year---even during tough times! One year, God spoke to me to give $1,000 per month to the Dream Center in Los Angeles of which Matthew Barnett was the pastor. At first, I told God that was unfair since Tommy Barnett (pastor of Phoenix First Assembly of God, one of the largest churches in America) was Matthew Barnett's dad. I reasoned that, since at that time $65,000 per day was going through those ministries, they did not need our money. God said, "Oh yeah? Who is your Dad?" Then I asked God, "Okay, if this is you, have Pastor Barnett mention $1,000 per month specifically." When he did, I asked a lady from our church, "What is God telling you our church should give?" She said, "$1,000 per month." It seemed I just could not get out of it.

When I went to our board meeting, the board agreed that it was right even though we were doubling our giving. Well, we gave almost every month, and at the end of the year still needed $20,000 to make the budget. I tried not to be discouraged, but instead, just prayed. To my amazement, the secretary called me in New York on December 30 and said, "Two businessmen just came in and asked if I could give them a receipt if they gave something today. They just gave me two checks totaling $42,000! Wow! You really can't out-give God!

Another principle was that of *praying specifically*. As God led people in the Bible, they often asked for exactly what they needed. For all of our ministries and activities, I ask people to come up with specific prayer lists so we can see God answer. The Bible says that we have not because we ask not. (James 4:2)

One time I wrote on my prayer list that I needed a laptop. Our district youth director gave me one. God led me to give that one away and I asked for a newer one. Another leader gave me their newer used laptop. God led me to give that one to a missionary in Uruguay. God asked me to be more specific so I asked for a Dell. My brother called me and informed me that his work was updating their computers and that he was buying me one. It was a Dell. As soon as I received it in the mail, God led me to give it to one of the leaders in the church. I felt God telling me to be more specific. I then asked for a Dell Inspiron 5150. The team from the Korean church came down again and before they left asked me if I needed anything. I said I did not know what to ask for. They said, "How about a laptop?" I said that I had been praying for one and even though I did not inform them what I was praying for, they sent me a Dell Inspiron 5150. Not only did they send that, but they sent an all-in-one printer too. Praise God!

As new missionaries, my wife and I had to pay self-employment tax. We were not familiar with this and ended up owing $868 that we did not have. We began to pray specifically for the $868. On the week of tax day, we still did not have the money. I encouraged Kim that God was going to provide. We were scheduled to speak at First Assembly of God in Walterboro, S.C. No one knew about our financial need. We did not know it, but the mission team had agreed not to receive an offering, but to give us $300 instead, which was a large sum compared to most of their missions offerings up to that point as a church. After I spoke, the pastor came to the pulpit weeping. He said that God had spoken to him and let him know that we had a special financial need and that the church should receive a love offering. They did, and it was $869.30---$1.30 more than what we needed! Praise God! He gave us enough to buy a soda on the way home!

In December of one year, the ministry had received only about $1,000 for the month. Our annual budget was $100,000, and until then only $95,000 or so had come in. I prayed and prayed, because, once again, the bills were due. I had to go to the District office on December 30th for something else. While I was there, I asked Brother Brown(our District Superintendent) for some financial help. I told him we needed $10,000. He said they really did not have it but that he and Brother Vic Smith (District Evangelism Director) would pray for me. They held hands in his office and prayed for me. As soon as they had prayed, I went to walk out of the office into the lobby and my phone rang. Our secretary, Helen, said, "Pastor Gordon, I had a very profitable lunch." I said, "Oh really? What happened?" She replied, "I had lunch with a lady from my church. She wanted to give some money to Hope." I said, "How much did she give?" She said, "10". I said sarcastically, "Great. Send her a receipt." Helen said, "No, Pastor. $10,000!" PRAISE GOD!

We needed the money right away. We prayed since the bank usually places holds on large sum checks like that. When Helen went to the bank, she asked if they would only place a partial hold on it. The lady said it would probably be at least a two-day hold. After she entered it into the computer, she had a look of surprise on her face. "I can't believe it", she said. "They are not placing any hold at all on it!! I do not understand!" We were able to access it immediately even though it was from another bank.

We constantly struggled financially. This kept me on my toes spiritually and kept me on my face before God. One time we could not pay our $800 rent bill. The day the rent was due I stayed home and spent the morning in prayer. On the way to the office, I stopped by the P.O. Box. There were two checks in the box. One check was for $100. The other check was from a family whose mother had been in the hospital and then passed away. I had been by to pray for her; her family was touched and sent me $700. Wow! The $800 (exactly) had come in!

A couple years later, I was in a meeting with some pastors. The need was greater this time. We needed $30,000. Our superintendent was there; I figured since it worked before I would ask him and the other pastors to pray. They did and then we left to go from the church to meet at a place for lunch. Enroute to the restaurant, the secretary called again. She said someone just walked in here and gave $30,000 in stocks to the church. Praise God again! We were able to liquidate them and use them for God's work!

When we went to Phoenix for Tommy Barnett's Pastor's School, many prayers were answered. One was that we would have a cheap place to stay. One of the cheaper hotels had rooms blocked off for $84 per night. I had waited too long. Every time I called, over the course of a few days, the man kept placing me on hold. When I finally reached him there were two rooms left at that rate, but while we were talking someone booked them over the internet. I said, "How about helping a brother out?" Even though he had placed me on hold so many times, he still refused to give us those rates. He claimed that $95 was the best he could do. He treated me very rudely and I was tempted to call his manager, but then I thought, "Why bother? He is probably having a rough day. And besides, I am to do unto others as I want to be done unto." I called other hotels, they were all booked, so I had to call back and reserve the expensive rooms. I prayed and called back. As soon as he knew who I was, he said, "I am going to help a brother out. I will give you rooms for $69!" PRAISE GOD! Cheaper than the blocked off rooms!

Provision of equipment was also miraculous. We never seemed to have enough money to buy things. I learned to write down specific prayer requests about equipment we needed. On one of our first lists, I wrote down a need for a bus, tables, a fax machine, and a locker. I prayed and prayed. One day I received a letter about a church that had burned down. One of their needs was an overhead projector. God spoke to me and told me to give this church one of our two overhead projectors. I complained because I knew they had good insurance and they had much more money than we had. I waited two weeks and God kept moving me to give it, so I boxed it up and sent it out. A couple of days later, a team came from Miami. They wanted a table to use for their display. When they found out I only had two tables in the church, the leader said, "Come with me." He escorted me to Office Depot and said, "I want to buy you a table and anything else you need." He bought us two tables, a fax machine and a locker. Then, that week, a church called us and donated a bus to us!

Additionally, we needed a hand truck and a CD player, so I wrote them down and began to pray. One Friday afternoon I was trying to prepare for a very busy week-end. Around three o'clock I began to feel sick. When I went home I had a 103 degree temperature. I had all the symptoms of the flu. I prayed for healing but still felt sick. I wanted to rest but the Lord told me to take my wife to an auction. I told her I wanted to take her because I would be busy that weekend and I knew she liked auctions. She said I was too sick to go. I told her I thought God wanted us to be there. The first thing that happened when we arrived there was that we were able to purchase a great hand truck and CD player at very low prices. I was excited but feeling very sick. The Lord spoke to me and told me to go witness to the teenager behind the counter. I walked over and began a conversation with him. He opened up and said that his parents were getting a divorce and his whole world was shaking. I shared the love of God with him and encouraged him to trust in Jesus. God touched his heart and we prayed. While I was walking back to my seat, I began to sweat. At that moment, my fever broke and I began to feel better. I recovered, overcoming the flu in just five hours!

One time, we moved our sound system and one of the people helping said we needed a 'snake'. I did not know what it was, so they explained that it was a long cord that had ways to connect microphones and musical instruments to the sound board from the stage. I placed it on my prayer list. One day I was cleaning out my garage and I found an old suitcase someone had given the church. Apparently, they must have given it to us with some sound equipment but I just assumed it was a suitcase. Well, anyway, I opened it up and was amazed to find a 'snake'! We used it for 10 years, having recently replaced it.

When we were building our men's house, we needed tile nippers. We did not have any time to pick some up, so we prayed. A man came out and said, "Look what I found inside the wall I was tearing down." It was a pair of tile nippers!

Sometimes we did not receive help we needed and I did not understand. Often, it turned out that there was a reason for it. I became frustrated one day because I could not pay off a credit card bill on the day I thought I needed to. I complained to God, reminding Him that He promised to provide. When I called the credit card company, they reminded me that I still had one more day. The money came in the next day and I was able to pay it on time.

Another time, I was frustrated with God because I needed to deposit money to keep checks from bouncing. I went to four different ATMs on Sunday afternoon and they were all broken. Again, I complained to God and reminded Him that He promised to help me. The next morning, I stopped by a bank branch. When I pulled up, I decided it would be faster to step inside the branch. I pled with the manager about putting the money in the bank with no penalties, explaining the problem I had with the ATMs. The manager checked his records and said that none of the ATMs had been down on Sunday. I was shocked. Then he informed me that if I had deposited the check that Sunday, it would not have even posted on Monday. He explained that it was a good thing that I had come in on Monday because I could cash the check, deposit the cash and then everything would be fine! God stopped me from doing the wrong thing! Amazing God!

As we put these principles to work, we saw God do many things. We learned to "cry out", pray according to His will, pray in righteousness, give to the poor, sow and reap, and pray specifically, and we saw results! Jesus said, "If you abide in Me, and my words abide in you, ask whatever you wish, and it will be done for you." (John 15:7)

OUTREACH PARTIES

Provision for outreaches was another amazing thing that happened over and over. We would sponsor outreach parties in the city, knowing that God asked us to give receptions and invite the poor. Most of the time, we did not know until the last minute where the resources were coming from, but God was always faithful.

Oh how God so wonderfully showed Himself faithful over these years of outreach! One of the areas he showed Himself faithful over and over was in the weather. Until recently (November, 2010), we have had 86 outreaches and have not been rained-out or on once! We had a 'parks and recreation' committee meeting and they asked what the rain plans were on the last two outreaches. I stated that we had not been rained on in 80 outreaches and I did not plan on rain; even though, on the last outreach there was a 100% chance of rain, it did not rain at our park until the outreach was over! Isn't God amazing! We also had sidewalk Sunday school in the housing projects every Saturday morning for about three years. Every week the team would meet and we would have a specific prayer list for the upcoming outreach. We would always pray about the weather, and during those three years it only rained once, when I was out of town.

One time, it had rained a lot the day before the outreach. It was still raining at 6pm on the night before while we began setup. The city parks and recreation people had said we could only have the basketball courts because it was supposed to rain that night and the next day. The park was already saturated and because it flooded there the field would be unusable. Well, we walked around the field seven times praying in the rain and Clayton (a man on staff at the church who had been saved at an outreach and is now directing our men's house) said, "What should we do, Pastor?" I said, "Set up the whole field. I am believing for no rain and that this field will be dry in the morning." Interestingly enough, the rain stopped and the wind began to blow and blew all night until the field dried out. At 7am the next day, the sun came out and we had a wonderful outreach distributing school supplies and uniforms to poor children.

One of the first outreaches we did involved a blanket tent meeting where we intended on distributing blankets. A man from Walterboro, a nearby town, offered to gather blankets for us. I handed out about 2000 flyers. As was our custom, we had a prayer list drafted, particularly for the outreach with specific requests. One was for the 200 blankets we claimed to be giving away. About a week and a half before the outreach, I asked the man how many blankets he had gathered. He said, "I think I have 4." I tried to be positive and not panic but I did not know what to do. We took it to the Lord in prayer.

A man named Johnny Tyrrell called me and asked if I wanted to go fishing. While speaking with him, the Holy Spirit said, "Ask him to speak at the blanket outreach." I did and he said, "What is it that you are doing?" When I explained, he said, "Do you need any more blankets?" I said, "Why yes." He said, "This is interesting. Just yesterday, St. Francis Hospital called to say they had a bunch of blankets to give away and they wanted to know if I knew of a non-profit group that could use them." We went up to the storage place and they had hundreds of blankets right there ready to go! Praise Jesus!

We had numerous miracles at our Christmas outreach on December 15, 2007! We had a specific prayer list that we used at all-night prayer on the week before the outreach.

Almost all of the requests were answered specifically! As we approached our outreach, the weatherman was saying the morning temperature would be 38 degrees and that it would probably rain. Well, just as we had specifically prayed from our prayer list, the temperature did not drop below 60 that night! It reached almost 70 and it did not rain until 1:30 pm, just as we were wrapping up! A lady who was going to bring horses was supposed to have surgery that week and could not make it, so we prayed that God would move. The hospital's malpractice insurance lapsed and they called and said they would have to postpone the surgery and the horses made it to the outreach! We prayed for 700 gifts and 700 kids. We had around 500 gifts for ages 4-13 and we had a few stuffed toys for kids under 4. We prayed specifically for stuffed toys for the kids. Amazingly, a lady had purchased 118 teddy bears in November and brought them on the night before the outreach, to bring us to about 700 gifts! When we handed out the gifts, the last gift went to the last child, so we had just enough! A MIRACLE! 700 gifts for 700 kids! 125 volunteers showed up, which was the exact amount we prayed for! We prayed for $2,000 for the outreach and sure enough, a lady from Redeemer Presbyterian Church brought by a check for $2,000 three days prior to the outreach. Because of this, we were able to contact Roarke Ferguson to see if he could bring his reptile zoo and, miraculously, he was able to come on short notice as we had prayed. Many children received Christ at the event as another answer to prayer!

We had prayed for unexpected blessings too! Edy's Ice Cream called and said that because some freezers broke down, they had a refrigerated truck full of ice cream to give away and they wanted to know if there was a non-profit group that could distribute the ice cream.

They showed up in their truck on Saturday and gave out just over 700 ice cream items including half-gallons and more! The food bank called two days before the event and wanted to know if we could give out frozen turkeys and dinners free. We distributed them to adults at the event!

The next miracle pertained to the 30 kids that attend King's Kidz Weekly. They were coming the following Thursday and by Wednesday we had no gifts and no money to buy them. God led me to give 30 gifts to kids in another inner-city ministry Wednesday night. I called our children's director and said, "Let's pray. The gifts are on the way!" Sure enough, I was on a conference call Thursday morning and people from Praise Assembly in Beaufort came by saying, "We have been collecting toys for your kids and we decided to bring them today!" I had no idea! Then, while I was still on the phone, a worker called. He was at Food Lion picking up free groceries and they asked him if we needed toys. They had been collecting them for an inner-city school, and while he was in the store, they called the school and found out it was closed for the holidays. They gave us the toys and we had an overabundance, just as we had prayed!

In 2009, we were going to host a Convoy of Hope. There was a location that we used before, which was one of the only ones big enough to stage the event. It was owned by The Navy Yard at Noisette which was going to redevelop it in conjunction with the City of North Charleston. I approached them about using the lot and they denied us. They said that they were going to be breaking ground on the site before October. I prayed about it and God showed me that we would be able to have the event there. I told our management team that "No" was the new "Yes". Everyone laughed, but I was serious.

A month later (three months before the event), there was an article in the local newspaper. It was about 'Noisette' being hit with foreclosure on a property. I figured this may slow them down and may have been allowed by God, so I called them. They denied us again because they said they were still hopeful to break ground before our event in October. Well, we prayed, and some fasted and prayed. After a couple of weeks, it became more apparent that their plans were on hold. I called again and they still denied us because they said the lot was being used by the police that weekend.

Finally, someone called the mayor's office and he agreed to talk to Noisette. Noisette ended up calling us. Not only did they let us use their lot but also more areas for parking. In addition, the mayor's office agreed to provide us with free dumpsters, stage, garbage cans, garbage trucks and more. Much of this would not have happened if we did not have the struggles we had. Praise God. What the enemy meant for evil, God turned around and used it for good---more than we could ask or think!

In 2009 we were supposed to have an Easter outreach. We had a problem with the city concerning obtaining a park permit. It was two weeks before the outreach and I was visiting in New York with my family. I felt that I needed to work on obtaining a park but God kept leading me to spend time with my family. He said, "You spend time with your family. Fast and pray this week and I will get you your park by Friday." I was a little nervous because this involved over 100 volunteers and 1,000 guests and I had no clue what was going to happen. I simply trusted and obeyed. On Friday at noon, my wife said, "Aren't you worried about having a park for the outreach?" I responded that I was not worried since God had spoken. About an hour later, a lady called me and said that she had the cell phone number of Wendell Gilliard, one of our representatives in state government. She said she felt that he could help me. I asked God if I should call this man and, of course, He responded with something like "Duh… What do you think?"

I called the representative and he asked me to call the parks and recreation director and put him on a three-way call. After hanging up on Wendell two times by accident, I finally connected the call. The man stated that he could try, but he was working on obtaining a grant and was busy. God said, "Fast until 4pm and you will have your park." At exactly 4:00 pm (I looked at my phone when it rang and it said exactly 4:00), the director called me and informed me that we could have Harmon field, which turned out to be a much better venue than we had ever used before!

In 2010 we were having a vision-casting luncheon for Convoy of Hope. I was battling as I was preparing for it. I felt that the Lord wanted it outside, so I began searching for a large tent to use for the 200 people who would come. It was about three weeks before the luncheon. We had prayed for many things such as a free tent, wonderful gourmet food, two businesses to sponsor it, a free table and chairs and more. Well, I began to discover that not only would no one give us a free tent, but there were no tents to be had in the Charleston area. It turned out that May is the biggest month for tent use in Charleston. A few companies told me that not only could they not give us a discount but they could not get us a tent even if we paid full price.

I tried not to panic. I considered calling the city of North

Charleston and moving the event indoors, but the Holy Spirit cautioned me, saying that He wanted it outside because that is where he wants His church reaching out. It was ten days before the event and we still did not have a tent. We did not have money or food. I was praying about some other things and felt a strong conviction to call my wife's cousin. As a pastor, he was between churches. He had just married and now he was living with his new wife and mother-in-law. I was convicted; even though I knew he was struggling, I had not called him to encourage him. The Lord began to chastise me about being too busy to really reach out in love.

I called my wife's cousin and began to encourage him. I asked about his plans. He mentioned that he was about to purchase a large tent to use for tent meetings. He said, "By the way, if you ever want to use it, you could use it for free." I said, "What? Free tent? How big is it?" It turned out to be large enough. A few days before the event, I picked it up on the way through Columbia, S.C. A breakthrough began to happen. Sixty pounds of fish were donated by one business and friends. Another business cooked the fish for free. We had 100 pounds of potatoes at the ministry center to use for potato salad. A church called and offered 100 pieces of fried chicken. We were given 60 pounds of chicken for free. A man bought enough hot dogs and offered to cook them. God provided everything we prayed for almost to the tee! In addition to all of that, we had another outdoor event with no rain, bringing our total to 85!

At that same Convoy of Hope event, we were having trouble finding a place for the event. I contacted people including state representative Gilliard who had helped us at the Easter event. He talked with the city about some green space where the old Cooper River Bridge used to be. He called me and met me there and said we had to wait until the following week because the Mayor was out of town. Our team met at the field and we prayed. God spoke to us telling us that "every place on which the soles of your foot treads, I have given it to you." (Joshua 1:3) We believed God was giving us that land. Two days later, I was praying in the morning and God said, "I am giving you a site for Convoy today and it is going to be the green space." I said, "But God, the Mayor won't be in until next week." That morning, when I finished praying, the representative called me and informed me that the city did not own the land. It was owned by the State Department of Transportation. Within a moment, he had the local SCDOT leader on the phone and they guaranteed us use of the land.

When we finally received the letter on a Friday confirming this, there were a lot of stipulations about the blocking of streets, the use of the land, and parking. Even with all God had done, I still had doubt. I called an emergency team meeting on Sunday afternoon, and really, because I did not want the hassle, was going to try to squirm out of the Convoy. While I was in church that morning, representative Gilliard called. Between services, I called him back. He said, "Is everything okay with that land? I was thinking about it this morning." I mentioned about the street blocking and parking. He replied, "Oh, don't worry about that, the city is going to help with all of that." Well, God answered that again.

Throughout the process of planning, I kept mentioning to the team that God had been speaking to me about David bringing the ark into the city. The first time they tried, they did not do it according to listening to God. The second time, they were more careful and preceded the moving of the glory into the city with praise and worship. I asked if they felt like they understood the meaning of it. No one did, but when the city decided we had to move the date, I understood. I believe God was giving us more time to celebrate correctly.

We moved the date to December 11 and decided to make it into a huge Christmas party. As we have been planning, God has been speaking about John the Baptist preparing the way for the glory of God. He also keeps telling us that everywhere we tread, God will give us the land. Interestingly enough, a prayer leader named our first prayer walk "Pre-praying the Way of the Lord." While there, one of our precious church members who used to be a heroine addict said, "Hey, God will give us everywhere our feet tread." I am very excited to see what God will do at this particular event!

THE FAMILY THAT PRAYS TOGETHER

I began to teach my children how to pray. One time, when my oldest daughter Kara was seven years old or so, we were selling candy bars door-to-door for her school. We had sold many one-by-one. We had never sold more than two at a door. It was almost night-time and I felt led to pray with Kara that at the next door we would sell the last three. We prayed, knocked and no one came to the door. I was discouraged and we walked away. We were well down the street when someone called out from that house. We went back and the man said he wanted to buy our last three candy bars!

We had a baptism at the beach and were driving there on our bus. It was raining. Kara said she wanted to pray that it would stop raining when we arrived at the beach and that it would not rain until we left. Everyone was amazed that when the first person stepped off the bus, it stopped raining. We stayed at the beach for a couple hours and it did not rain. It started raining as soon as everyone was on the bus again! Wow! God is good!

One time I took my two youngest daughters to the beach. I told them that I felt like we should trust God for some things for our trip. They said they wanted to pray to see a whole starfish, a live horseshoe crab, a jellyfish, some kind of large shell we had not seen before, a shark's tooth, and that it would not rain. Well, it did not rain and we found everything we prayed for even though we had never found a whole starfish or a live horseshoe crab at this beach before. The only thing we did not find was a shark's tooth. Autumn asked why and I said it was because sometimes we have to wait on God. Two days later, we had a guest speaker at our church and a friend came up to me. Somehow we ended up on the subject of shark's teeth. He said that he had found a good place to find shark's teeth. Within a week, we went together and found 25 of them and I was able to remind Autumn of the goodness of God.

Another time, we were at my parents' house in New York. We went on a nature hike and I asked the kids what we should trust God for. They said they wanted to see a deer up close. I prayed also for a snake and they kept saying they did not want to see a snake. I told them that even though we had never seen a snake on one of our many nature hikes at my parents' house, I felt we needed to pray to see one. The Spirit led me to turn over a rock but God said that when I did I needed to be ready to jump back. I did and out jumped a snake. I caught it, brought it to the house, and we named it 'Scooter'.

Kim and I had agreed before we were married that we would have three children. When Kara was born with cystic fibrosis, a genetic disease, Kim decided she did not want to have any more children. I could not accept this, so I began to pray for another child. I prayed and prayed. As soon as Kara was old enough, I asked her if she wanted a sibling. She said she wanted a younger sister. Every night as I tucked Kara in, she and I would pray (without Mom knowing!) for a little sister. When Kara was six years old, Kim came in the living room and said, "Kara and I have a surprise for you! I am pregnant!" Of course it was little Sara! Praise God for hearing our petitions!

Since Kim and I agreed on three children, I began to pray again for another. Kara and Sara were six years apart and I did not know what God was going to do. I prayed and prayed. Kim's sister had a young foster child named Autumn. At one time, Kim and I discussed the fact that if Autumn was ever up for adoption we could adopt her. We found out, after a couple of years, that she was eligible for adoption, so we began the process and paperwork.

She moved in with us as a foster child. She lived with us for about a year and then we had to go to court for a hearing to terminate the parental rights of her grandmother who had custody. We were anticipating a real struggle. The grandmother had had parental rights for some of Autumn's siblings and cousins. Because she had the right to, every time her rights were terminated, she would appeal within six months which was her right. This process would be repeated and some of the children were never adopted because they reached the age of 18 before the rights were terminated. The night before the hearing, we happened to be speaking at a church in Lake Wylie where the pastor was also in the adoption process. The church surrounded us and prayed fervently.

We went to court the next morning. The grandmother and her lawyer were in the lobby with us waiting with a bunch of other people who were there for other court issues. As we prayed, her lawyer came over and said, "My client says she would be willing to relinquish parental rights if you would be willing to grant her visitation during major holidays of the year." Wow! If she relinquished, then she had no right to appeal the decision and it would be final! Since we were going to keep in touch with the grandmother anyway, due to her poor health, and also that Autumn already knew her as her grandmother, we agreed. Court went well and everything was settled without a hitch! Praise God!

CHAPTER 4

CHANGED LIVES: SOMETHING FROM NOTHING

The most important and exciting way that we have seen God move in inner-city Charleston is in changing people's lives. One great aspect about inner-city ministry is that you have a chance to see many people's lives radically changed. Jesus met people where they were. While others ignored hurting people and the poor, Jesus went to the afflicted to serve them. He came to preach good news to the poor and bind up the brokenhearted. In Bible times, lepers in Israel had to shout "Unclean!" when others came by. Instead of running away from them, even though their uncleanness was so apparent, Jesus walked to them and said, "I will place my hand on your leperous wound and love you and heal you!"

As we went forth with Jesus' model of ministry, we were constantly amazed at the potential in people's lives. A man and a woman were living in a crack-house near the church. They began coming to the church and we ministered to them. One day my wife saw a man beating up the woman on a street behind the church. She stopped the car so our new friend could get in, and then the man rode his bike to her car and began threatening them. My wife called me and I grabbed two of the biggest men from the church I could find and ran over. The police came and eventually caught the man and we went to court and helped this new church member.

The couple kept attending the church and God delivered them from drugs. They came to my Hope Group (neighborhood Bible study) and we began to teach them how to pray. One day I said, "If you delight in God, He will give you the desires of your heart. What are your dreams?" He said that his dream was having a car and his CDL (license) and to drive trucks for a living again. She said she wanted to finish school. Well, all of this happened within two years!

Unfortunately one day, after he had been working for a while, he went in to work and there was a chain on the fence and no one was there. The business had closed with no warning and the workers were not paid for the last work they had done. Since the couple was living from paycheck to paycheck, they were concerned about their bills. They came to Hope Group and requested prayer. I told them that we had no funds to help but that we would pray and I believed the Lord would provide.

The following Tuesday the wife came to our morning devotions. When the time came for discussion she said, "I am here because God is real! I cannot believe what happened! We went to pay our light bill and when we opened it, we discovered we owed $0! We went to pay the water bill, and it was $1.47! We went to pay the rent and the landlord said that since we had stayed there long enough, we owed $200 less that month! Praise God! He provided for our needs in a miraculous manner!" He received a job soon after that and they continued on praising the Lord.

Another couple was living under a bridge. They had been struggling with crack addiction for years. They had been married 27 years. They started coming to the church and God began to touch and rebuild their lives. They stopped using drugs and the man started working. They moved into an apartment down the street. They joined my discipleship/study group. One evening I asked everyone what their dreams were.

They said that their dream was four-fold. They wanted their children back in their lives; they wanted to renew their vows; they wanted wedding rings which they had never had; and they also wanted their children to volunteer at Convoy of Hope. As we prayed daily for these dreams, miracles began to happen. First, their children started to call them and relate to them again. As they corresponded, they invited them to volunteer at Convoy of Hope. The children, who were from another town, said yes. On the weekend of Convoy, the church paid for a hotel room for their 9 kids and 13 grandkids. They volunteered at that Saturday outreach. Then Sunday, they cooked a meal for the church. After church we were going to have a renewing-of-the-vows service for them. I asked if they had wedding rings. The husband said the rings had not arrived as yet, but they were on the way. He spoke in faith because their children had not bought them rings as gifts like they thought they would. While starting the ceremony, the sound system experienced technical difficulties, so I stepped down from the stage and was speaking to someone about it. A lady came up to me and said, "Pastor, I did not know you were doing a renewing of the vows. Do you think this couple could use these?" She pulled out two of the most beautiful wedding rings I have ever seen. I snuck them into my coat pocket and during the ceremony surprised them. What a MIRACLE! Everyone began to weep with joy as we watched what God did to honor marriage. PRAISE GOD!

One day, a young lady came to our church because she needed groceries. She decided to start coming to church. She was really struggling. She lived in the housing projects. She had two children. She struggled because she was not able to keep a job. It seemed that every time she found a job, she ended up rebelling against her boss and being fired. As she continued to come, she entered discipleship. She was doing drugs, dealing drugs and living a promiscuous life. As her heart began to open up towards the Lord, she admitted that she had been molested as a child. Her mother would have different men living in the home and sometimes they would take advantage of her as a child. She said she tried to talk to her mom about it, but never succeeded. At night, she would not sleep because she was scared. She would write letters to her mom about her feelings, but never give them to her.

All of this made her hurt, bitter and rebellious. She masked the hurt with drug use and expressed the bitterness and rebellion in her relationships, especially with authorities. At the church, she surrendered her life to Christ. As she began to realize the source of her problems, she forgave. She began to learn to trust again. Eventually, she took another job. She was able to keep it. God began to move her up. She moved to a better one and a better one and now works for a lab company. She met a man at work and he began to come to church. Eventually, they were married at the church. She is now the director of the nursery and he is an usher. Praise God!

One college student came to our church for a year. He had been struggling because he grew up in an abusive home. When the summer came, he told me he was going to go back to his home. I had been discipling him, so I recommended that home might not be the best place for him because of the abuse and the unhealthy family environment. He claimed that he needed to go because he had nowhere to stay and no vehicle. I said, "Let's ask God for a vehicle and a place where you can stay." A man from our church came and said he wanted to give this student a car! We discovered a place for him to stay. He still left, but after recently hearing from him, he has decided to come back. Praise God!

A young man came to our church because his father brought him to receive food. His father had a drug problem. As a result, he and his father had lived in abandoned houses for eight years! I noticed that he became very faithful and teachable. I began to meet with him and disciple him. He had only been to one church service in his life. When we began to study the Bible, he did not even know what the chapters and verses were. He opened his heart up to Jesus and God began to bless his life. The church became a family to him. He learned that the people he spent time with affected his life. I began to encourage him to hang out at the church instead of spending time on the streets with his dad's drug-addicted and alcoholic friends.

Eventually, God provided him with a part time job. He was a hard worker just like his dad and soon gained another part time job. He was able to obtain an apartment. Now he works full time at a local attraction. He is a 'daily deacon' at the church when he is not working. As people come in for help, he is able to talk to them and help them with resources from the church.

One man came to our church who was addicted to crack and heroine. He had tried to attend one church when he was suicidal, but they asked him to leave because he was dirty and not dressed properly. He came to our church to receive a free ham he was going to sell on the street. God touched him and he started coming more regularly. As he was discipled and grew in Christ, he was involved in a '12-step program'. God cleaned him up. He was a great worker with a great attitude and God blessed him with a good job. After nine years, he is still blessed. He works as our head usher.

Another man came to a Convoy of Hope. He had, also, almost never attended church. He was homeless and addicted to crack, alcohol and methamphetamines. When he came to the ministry tent, he received Jesus as Savior. He asked for extra prayer because of his addictions. When he was prayed for, he felt a warmth and tingling he never felt before and that was the last time he ever used drugs! He began coming to church and being faithful. God slowly delivered him from alcohol and then cigarettes.

He was working in construction. When he learned about tithing he decided to 'try it'. When he did, he received a $1 per hour raise that week. He tried it the next week and received another $1 raise. When he was not at work, I encouraged him to come work at the church to stay busy so he was not around the friends he used to party with. One day, he went to load up the van and I threw him the keys. The Lord told me that he was going to receive a vehicle. I told him and he remarked that it would not do any good since he owed so much money to the DMV in California. I told him that God would not give him a vehicle unless he intended for him use it. Sure enough, the next week he came in and said, "Guess what? My boss gave me a truck." He went to check at the DMV and they said he did not owe anything and to go ahead and get his license!

Recently (August, 2010), he knocked the bumper off a car with one of our vans. He came in the office with tears in his eyes because he felt so badly about it. He did not want our church insurance to go up. Apparently, the owner of the vehicle could not be found so he left a note on the car. I said, "Clayton, don't worry! Let us pray that God will keep this out of court and it will be fixed for cheap." We held hands and prayed. He came in later that day, once again with tears in his eyes. These were tears of joy. The lady had just called him. She informed him not to worry because nothing was wrong with her car. He told her what happened and she said the bumper was fine. She said, "If the bumper falls off, I will call you. It is okay right now." WOW! As he grew, God blessed him. He is now on staff at the church caring for many pastoral duties, the men's house, and is also in our Bible institute.

Another lady came to an outreach who was struggling with manic depression. She was afraid to drive and afraid to go out into the community. She would walk to work, walk home and then sit with her visually impaired husband with the shades down and the door locked. She would watch tv and smoke cigarettes. We had an outreach on the street behind the church and she came. She surrendered to God and started attending church. Over the years, as God worked on her heart, she forgave many people who had hurt her. Her doctor eventually took her off the seven medications she was on. She stopped smoking. She bought a truck and began driving to church. Now, she runs the clothing ministry and drives the vans to give people rides to and from church!

After she came to the church for a few months, she asked for prayer for her feet. She had to wear orthopedic shoes and the job she had was hard on her feet. God spoke to me and said, "Tell her if everywhere she goes she shares good news, encouragement, the gospel and love, I will heal her feet. How blessed are the feet of him who brings good news." I told her and we prayed for her and over the period of a few weeks, her feet were healed! They have been fine for seven years now!

One man came off the streets. He had been waiting on the steps of a church in Charleston's east side, hoping someone would invite him to church. When they had church, they would just ask him to leave so they could use the steps. When he came to our church, I just put him to work. He was a large fellow, so I asked him to be a head-greeter and sort of a 'blessed bouncer.' He was a great person. The more he came, the stronger he became in the Lord. Unfortunately, he started living with a woman. I told him that was wrong and they could not be members. They were offended and left, but later came back and asked me to do marriage counseling with them. They were married four years ago in our church. He has been clean and sober for seven years now! He leads a Bible study and his wife leads a kids dance team at the church!

A lady came to our first service as a church. She was addicted to crack and alcohol. She came regularly, but struggled. One day, her house was broken into and she was shot six times. She actually survived. She started to come to church more regularly. Now, she does not do drugs any more. She heads up "ministry Fridays", where people come to do work to prepare for the weekend activities. God has blessed her and she continually comes and serves at the church.

Another man came about a year ago. He was on the verge of being homeless. All he had to wear were 'sweats' and he was separated from his wife. Although he was very active in the recovery community, he had never been part of a church. We began the discipleship process. Today, he is back with his wife and he constantly brings testimonies of miracles in his life. God has blessed him financially as he has learned to give. He has remarkable wisdom and knowledge of the Word. He is about to take over our Thursday night Christian 12-step program!

One day, a man was working for the city and he came by and swept the front of the church. I watched how diligent he was. It was cold out so I brought him a cup of coffee and encouraged him with what a great work he was doing. He started coming to the church. Because he was addicted to crack, he entered our men's house. He was there for a while, but left. Our men's house director went out and found him and he came back. Today he has been clean for a couple of years and is acting as a ministry deacon and usher in the church!

CHAPTER 5

REVIVAL

Many people have claimed that revival is coming to Charleston, South Carolina and I believe it. Many things appear to be bringing us to it, but so far it has not come.

America needs revival. In 1991, church attendance was at 49%. In 2002, it was 43%. From 1992–1999, the population of the United States grew by 9%. Church attendance dropped by 12% during that same period. Two-thirds of U.S. churches are plateaued (in attendance) or declining.[3] Only revival can bring the church back to life. As 'salt' and 'light', churches are really to be the leaders of their communities. Leadership is servanthood. Christians should be the biggest servant organizations in the neighborhoods---and the country.

As I studied church history, I became interested in revival. Most Christians want revival. Was it just prayer that invited the Holy Spirit to a location? Was it holiness? Was it unity? It seemed as though some of these were factors. Perhaps it was a combination? Whatever happened, there was a general pattern, like that found in the Bible. First, *there was a direction to seek God*. Like Jesus during His temptation, like the disciples in the book of Acts, like Josiah and his reforms, God called people to seek His face. As they did, the glory of God fell and then people were reconciled to God. We cannot forget that this is the end-result, and I believe a chief indicator, that revival has truly come. Souls are saved! Jesus said, "…

you will receive power when the Holy Spirit has come upon you; and you shall be My WITNESSES..." (Acts 1:8) He said, "Follow Me, and I will make you fishers of men."(Matthew 4:19)

Think about it. After Jesus fasted in the wilderness, seeking God, He was anointed with the Spirit. What did He immediately begin to do?---Preach good news to the poor, bind up the brokenhearted, proclaim the year of the Lord's favor. (Luke 4:18–19; Isaiah 61) He came to seek and save the lost. He began to act as the physician to the sick. On the Day of Pentecost, the disciples were seeking God, then they were empowered, and then they won souls. Josiah sought God, read His Scriptures, and then many turned to God. The temple was built to be a place where people who were having difficulties could come and find God, repent of their sins, and see God heal their land.

What was Jesus' ministry all about? Was he trying to build a big building? Was he spending time reaching those who were already in the Temple serving God? Was he selling books or trying to build a great choir? Was he holding lock-ins with the religious kids? Did he spend hours studying the intricacies of Scripture and ministry with His friends, but never let an outsider in? How did He spend His time?

Jesus' ministry was that of seeking and saving the lost. It was that of finding people who were sick physically or spiritually and bringing healing to them. It was walking the streets with the disciples and finding people on the fringe of society to let them know it was the time of God's favor and that their broken hearts could be mended. Even when he was spending his time with the disciples, he was talking about the harvest and training them to go out and find souls.

The majority of people in our ministry would not be there if we had not left the building and hit the streets with the Good News! We visited one man, weekly, through Without Walls for 18 months. He was always friendly but never shared a need. One day he was sick. That week, I visited him at work to make sure he was okay. A few weeks later, he mentioned that he would like a full-size refrigerator. I said, "You know what we do when we have a need? We pray that God will provide and He does." He, my friend from the Presbyterian Church and I held hands in his doorway and prayed for the fridge. When we arrived back at the church, we opened the back door and there was a refrigerator! To this day, no one knows where it came from or who it belonged to.

The Presbyterian friend grabbed the refrigerator and put it on his truck and brought it to his apartment. A couple weeks later, this man called me and said he lost his job due to an alcohol problem and that he really wanted help. We got him in the men's house. A few weeks later he said, "I want to pray for a guitar." We prayed together and within a week a man came by and gave us a guitar! Then he said, "I need an amp." We prayed and, sure enough, our Presbyterian friend came by with the amp. One night at all-night prayer, he said, "I am tired of chronic back pain. Will you pray for me?" We laid hands on him and prayed and his back was healed and it has felt a lot better since! None of this would have happened in his life had we not left the building, the four walls, and hit the streets---more than once.

Most revivals had certain things in common. We all know prayer and fasting were a significant part of them. I believe most people understand that holiness was a great part. *Revivals are born in a prayer meeting.* The move of the Spirit called people to repentance that led to holiness. Many people think that if we seek God through fasting and prayer and call people to repentance, we will see revival. But why has revival not come with all of the prayer and fasting going on today? I believe there are other factors that bring revival.

Yes, I know that people say that revival is a sovereign act of God and, in part, I believe it. I do not, however, believe that God just decides one day to send His manifest presence somewhere. I see revival coming in response to a certain atmosphere that welcomes God's precious Holy Spirit. In his book, *Total Forgiveness*, R. T. Kendall reminds us that the Spirit is a gentle dove.[4] Doves are known to be gentle and peaceful. They fly away in response to any disturbance, loud noise or conflict. He tells a story about a couple who became missionaries to Israel. When they moved there, a dove came to their home and made a nest on their roof. They felt it was a sign from God. The only problem was that the dove was not always there. When they raised their voices, slammed doors, or stomped around, the dove would fly away. They finally realized that they would have to love one another or the dove would fly way. The greatest influence inviting the blessed Holy Spirit to any church, organization, city or nation is love. Not just love and passion for God, but love and passion for others. The resting and remaining of the Holy Spirit Dove upon a certain place or organization is the seal of approval from God

How is this love and passion shown? One way is *unity*. On the day of Pentecost, the disciples were "all with one accord" (Acts 2:1, KJV). Jesus' teaching and high priestly prayer emphasized unity. (John 17) I believe we cannot represent who God is without a group of people serving

Him together.

Together, not alone, we make up His body. Jesus prayed that we would be one even as He and the Father are one. This means when Christians are united, God is glorified in a greater way because people see us represent Him more for Who He is---Three in One.

This emphasis on unity can be seen in historic revivals. D. L. Moody claimed that there was not a denominational bone in his body. William Booth united the church around the Great Commission and the Great Commandments. John Wesley and George Whitefield cooperated in the harvest fields even though their theological perspectives were opposite. They both reached out to people of different races. The Pentecostal revival at Azusa Street was characterized by unity among races as well as economic and denominational backgrounds.

How else is this love shown that welcomes the Holy Spirit and provides an atmosphere where He is welcome? Another factor that is common in revivals is 'care for the poor'. We can pray all we want, but the Bible says that if we close our ears to the cries of the poor, God will close His ears to our prayers. Isaiah 58 is a great reminder to us that even if we fast and pray, God will not hear us unless we open our hand to the poor and homeless. Unfortunately, I have found that most Christians today do not personally care for the poor. I understand this because during my first five years as a Christian, this was not in my scope of thinking. As a matter of fact, I do not remember a homeless person in the first two churches I attended, each of which had an attendance of over 500 people.

John the Baptist prepared the way for Jesus. He fasted and prayed outside the church building and religious structure. He called the people to repent. How were they to repent? "Let the man who has two tunics share with him who has none; and let him who has food do likewise." (Luke 3:11) He told tax collectors not to cheat people and be selfish and take too much from them. He told soldiers not to force people to give them money. He prepared a way for Jesus' anointing to come---not just by uniting people, worshipping, fasting and praying. He stood up for the rights of the poor and brokenhearted.

When revival is mentioned, many people think of the evangelistic campaigns and small house-group Methodist Societies of John Wesley. They may not be familiar with his emphasis on helping the poor. "John Wesley… campaigned for prison and labor reform, encouraged the building of orphanages and schools, battled against the slave trade, gave medicines and health treatment to the poor, worked to help resolve unemployment, set up accounts for making loans to the poor, and personally gave away considerable sums of money to people in need. Wesley exhorted his middle-class followers, 'If those who gain all they can, will likewise give all they can, then, the more they gain, the more they will grow in grace, and the more treasure they will lay up in heaven.' and 'There is no holiness but social holiness. There is no gospel but the social gospel.'"[5]

FREEMASONRY

At a conference I recently attended, Earl Creps asked some convicting questions that I believe lead us back to the primary purposes of our existence as a church. The questions were, "How many of the new people in the church are ones we have won and disciple? When was the last time you had a conversation with a poor person and what did you learn? If you had worked as a missionary for the Assemblies of God, would you still have a job?" The mark of a minister is not how he treats the highest and most important people, but how he treats the lowest.

Jesus cared for the *weak, small and unnoticed* ones. Jesus noticed when the widow's mite fell into the offering plate. He notices when the sparrow falls. He used the boy who only had five loaves and two fishes. Jesus cared for the ones who no one else wanted. I am a firm believer that if we go after the ones no one wants, God will give us the ones everyone wants. I believe we could see the greatest revival in history today. It will not be one with flashy evangelists and television ministries! It will happen on the streets, among the poor, as it always has since Jesus' ministry.

What will happen will be similar to what happened in the ministries of George Whitefield and John Wesley. Although they were theologically at opposite ends of the spectrum, they cooperated in ministry to the lost, poor and hurting. They brought their ministries out of the church and into the streets and concentrated on souls. They preached on the streets, started orphanages, fed people, worked for labor reform, and rallied people against slavery. They cared about social justice and lost souls.

An important part of Wesley's ministry was the small group, "Methodist Societies." They met in homes and in the 'marketplace'. They did not try to replace the church, but united the Christians in prayer, worship, and practical ministry. Wesley constantly taught his people to gain money to give to the poor. He encouraged them to stay faithful to their local churches.

About a year after I began ministry in Charleston, I had a dream. In that dream two strange-looking animal heads were trying to speak to me. One was a goat head. Another looked something like a cat. In my dream, I realized that they were demonic powers. In previous years, when confronted by demons in the night, I simply rebuked them and prayed for a while. When I felt peace and that I had the victory, I would go back to sleep. In my dream, I was able to forbid these demons to speak to me, but when I awoke I was overwhelmed with an evil presence. I prayed and prayed and could not seem to attain the victory. It was one of the most unsettling nights of my life.

It was not until around 10 years later that I began to understand the significance of the dream. In March of 2009, my mother was in the hospital and I was with her in New York. My friend, Assistant Pastor George Kugblenu, from Emmanuel Baptist Church on James Island, had given me some papers on Freemasonry about a year earlier. I decided to read them while in the room with my mother. I learned that the Knights Templar, precursors of the Freemasons, had been involved in the worship of a god named Baphomet. As soon as I read that, the Lord said to me, "There's your goat-demon." I immediately searched the internet and, sure enough, as I looked up Baphomet, I saw that he was represented as a man's body with a goat head or a goat head surrounded by a pentagram.

I began to realize that I was not just fighting a battle for individuals' lives that were oppressed by the devil. I was actually battling territorial demonic powers for the freedom of the Spirit's move in our city. I understand now why one of the first things God asked me to do when I moved to Charleston was to read about the history of the area. This became a key to understanding how to approach ministry. It turned out that Charleston was one of the most prominent cities in the development of the Scottish Rite of Freemasonry. The first Mother Supreme Council of the Scottish Rite of Freemasonry was actually in Charleston, S.C. until it moved to Washington, D.C.

One day I went to meet with the mayor of Charleston for a few minutes in one of his "nights out" (one-on-one citizen time). While waiting, a teacher from a Muslim temple approached me and began to oppose me. He talked about how we do not need a savior. He was arguing with me about Jesus not being God and about other things. Apparently, he must have known who I was because he kept trying to engage me in a quarrel. After my meeting, I told our secretary what had happened.

Two months later, I was going to the mayor's office again. The secretary said, "I think the Lord is telling me you are going to run into that Muslim issue again." I went to the waiting area and we were ushered into the office of the secretary of the mayor. When I walked in, I was surprised to see not only the Muslim teacher, but also a few city and county officials. The Muslim man began to speak about not needing a savior again. Then, interestingly enough, he began to speak about Freemasonry. He said to one city official, "You are a Freemason, aren't you?" He responded, "Yes". He asked the other two the same question and they responded affirmatively. Then he asked another one, "You are 33rd degree, right?" He responded, "Yes." Then the Muslim said, "Isn't it amazing the truth you learn at the 33rd degree? It is wonderful, isn't it?" From the studying I have done about Freemasonry, I understand that it is at the 33rd degree that people are taught that the god behind all of the other gods' names used is that of Lucifer.[6] There may be other lessons as well..........

A few months later, I was in my car and the Lord led me to listen to a CD that Pastor George Kugblenu had given me. I began to listen and then my kids began to talk, so I turned it off. I tried later, but some people entered the car and began talking to me, so I turned it off again. Later, my kids took it out to listen to one of their CDs. Finally, late that afternoon the Lord spoke to me and said, "Gordon, I have been telling you to listen to that CD and you have not. I want you to sit in your car in the parking lot and listen to it today. Listen now. You need to understand Freemasonry." Well, I sat in the car and listened to it.

After listening to the CD by Bill Suddeth explaining how Freemasonry was incompatible with Christianity, I went into my office and checked my email. In my email was a note from Joanne Parrott, who was working with our House of Prayer. She mentioned that a 32nd degree Mason was coming to visit and wanted to speak to Pastor George and me. Of course my curiosity was piqued. The next morning I was reading my Bible and the Lord had me stop and study about Hiram, King of Tyre. I did not know why.

About an hour later, this gentleman showed up in my office with Pastor George. He began to tell us that he had surrendered his life to Jesus and was not sure if he should do both Freemasonry and Christianity. Due to my crash course in Freemasonry and Pastor George's extensive knowledge, and due to the leading of the Holy Spirit, we were able to reason with him. He even mentioned Hiram (King of Tyre) and I was able to refute the false teaching he had been under. He was quite surprised by our knowledge (as was I). We praised God when he left the office with a commitment to leave Freemasonry and take as many people with him as possible. We are still waiting to see the fruit of our conversation. GOD IS AMAZING! HE ORDERS OUR STEPS!

Not long after that, we discovered that a man named Selwyn Stevens was coming from New Zealand to the United States. He happened to be an expert on Freemasonry and had experience in helping people get out of this group. He also had a ministry of dealing with the spirit of Freemasonry in certain territories. We decided to invite him to come and address Christians in our city and teach about Freemasonry. One of the facts that he mentioned was that every major move of God in history has involved a confrontation of Freemasonry. I have sensed that there is a major move of God coming to Charleston and I feel this is a necessary step in clearing the air for the approaching revival.

Whatever brings revival, we know it is greatly needed in America today. I believe it is possible. Some say that the United States will not be a superpower by the end times because they do not see it anywhere in the Bible, especially the book of Revelation. If this is true, it means either one of two things. It could be that America has suffered so greatly under the curse of God for disobedience that it has shrunk in its influence. Another possibility, however, could be that there would be so many believers at the time of the rapture, that the country is emptied and there are few people left.

CHAPTER 6

WITHOUT WALLS: THE HOUSE OF PRAYER

As I was involved in ministry in Charleston, God began a series of events that allowed me to know that He wanted to multiply what we were doing in Charleston in reaching impoverished neighborhoods and bringing love and discipleship. Any ministry in the church starts with prayer. It has been our philosophy that each ministry in the church should have a prayer ministry behind it. The house of prayer obviously starts with prayer. Prayer meeting ought to be the most important meeting in the church. To raise the level of a fleet of ships in the harbor, you must raise the level of the harbor.

God said He wanted His house to be a House of Prayer for all people. When the temple was dedicated, Solomon prayed that it would be a place for people to find God. It was to be particularly for those who were struggling and in sin. In II Chronicles 6, he prayed that if the people were defeated before their enemies; they had no rain; were experiencing famine, sickness, plague or locusts; were under some other curse due to their disobedience: then the temple would be a place for them to seek God and repent and receive forgiveness, healing and restoration. God answered that prayer in II Chronicles 7:14 when He said, "If my people, which are called by my name, shall humble themselves, and pray, and seek My face, and turn from their wicked ways; then will I hear from heaven, and will forgive their sin, and will heal their land." (KJV)

The temple was to be a 'soul-saving station' for 'all people.' This is the call for any house of prayer. Places where God is worshipped are to be healing stations for those who do not know God or are in trouble with God. They are to be places for people who do not know how to come to God and have an encounter with Him. God said in Isaiah 56: 6-8, "Also, the foreigners who join themselves to the Lord, to minister to Him, and to love the name of the Lord, to be His servants, everyone who keeps from profaning the sabbath, and holds fast My covenant; Even those I will bring to My holy mountain, and make them joyful in My house of prayer. Their burnt offerings and their sacrifices will be acceptable on My altar; for My house will be called a house of prayer for all the peoples. The Lord God, who gathers the dispersed of Israel, declares, 'yet others I will gather to them, to those already gathered.' "

At the time of Jesus' earthly ministry, the temple had a court for the Gentiles who were seeking God to encounter Him. I believe this was planned by God to fulfill His ultimate purpose, for people to be saved; for people who did not know Him to come to Him. Unfortunately, the people of God were not respecting that. They were selling animals for sacrifice in that court. They were exchanging money, telling the Gentiles that they had to use Jewish money and then charging them a fee. They were using the court as a place to pass through the city. It was all about their profit and gain and not about the lost being saved. There was clutter and confusion.

In walks Jesus. Jesus came to "seek and save the lost." He

came for the sick and not the well.

He did not come to use the people who were seeking God for their own gain. He came to serve and to draw the lost, hurting and lonely into the family of God. He came to bind up the brokenhearted and proclaim God's love and favor. When He saw this house of prayer, reconciliation and healing full of clutter and busyness and selfishness, He became angry. He grieved that they had made it a "den of thieves" and He turned over their tables and ran them out.

Instead of struggling and striving to utilize God's house to gain earthly wealth, the people of God should be striving and praying to help the lost gain eternal life. This is the contrast between a ministry that is truly seeking and saving the lost and committed to the Great Commission and the great Commandments, and a ministry that is trying to 'grow' and 'expand' in a constant effort to gain bigger buildings and budgets by grabbing up people who are already at other churches. God's emphasis has always been on people---not money and buildings.

I liken it to the difference between the TV shows *Love Boat* and *Deadliest Catch*. The people on the *Love Boat* are happy and finding love with one another on the boat. Things are pristine and perfect. They are not concerned with fishing. That would 'mess-up' their atmosphere. They may be interested in marketing their cruises to influence others who might do business with another cruise line to join them. On *Deadliest Catch*, the people are concerned with fishing for crabs. They are focused on the harvest and bringing it from outside of the boat to the inside. It is 'messy'. There does not seem to be enough help. They put in long hours and sacrifice for bringing in the harvest. This is what we should be doing for the harvest.

Unfortunately, when looked at truthfully, many churches are not fishing boats, they are cruise ships. If a church is not truly winning souls, it is not a church, it is a club. This has to change. Jesus said He came to seek and save the lost. Often, it is the religious trappings that turn the lost off when they come to church.

The people in the church can turn off the lost and keep them from being saved as well. On more than one occasion, someone came to me and said, "We should not hand out groceries in Sunday service. Many of the people come just to receive food." I always ask them, "What made you come to our ministry center for the first time?" Every one of them had come for food, clothing, a Mother's Day gift or something of the like. Instead of criticizing, they ought to be asking others to come to their small group, or asking them to engage in discipleship. I rarely am turned down when I ask a brokenhearted person to meet with me weekly over a cup of coffee.

Early on in our ministry, I found myself continually searching for income. One day God reminded me that if I would concentrate on winning souls, He would pay me. I believe that God will support a ministry that is focused on winning the lost and on discipleship. On a Sunday afternoon, I was praying in the church wondering how we were going to pay our bills. Along came a knock at the door. A man who I had met before came in. He was all scratched up and dirty and his clothes were torn. Apparently, he and his girlfriend had had a fight and she scratched him noticeably, so he hit her with a baseball bat. He was forced to leave the apartment and wanted me to help him with a place to stay and a meal. At first I was reluctant, knowing that we did not have the finances and also knowing that I did not want to help a man that would hit his girlfriend like that. God began to speak to me. He said, "I will tell you how to pay your bills. Take this man to a restaurant and buy him a nice meal. Then pay for a hotel room for him. Remember, I am kind to evil and ungrateful men (like you). Also, place your missions pledge money from your church in the mail." I hesitated for a moment. "God," I prayed, "why are You being so irresponsible. Don't You know what this man has done? Don't You know my church has bills to pay." After God reminded me that it was His church and His money, I relented and obeyed.

When I arrived home, a pastor friend had called me. I called him back that afternoon and he recounted a story that sounded all too familiar. He said, "Our church could not pay its bills. I prayed and God instructed me to receive a missions offering. I did not know who it was for. It was a good sized offering. After that we received the regular offering and it was the largest we ever had. We were able to pay our bills. This afternoon, while I was praying, God spoke to me and said this offering was for your church!" Amazing! All I had to do was help this man and be concerned about winning the lost around the world and God took care of the rest!

This is God's heartbeat. It has been from the beginning---to seek and save the lost. Unfortunately, churches that have been around for a while have sacred cows---those things that are taking up money and space but are not producing souls. Yes, there are programs that are good and events that are a blessing and that encourage 'church growth'. However, many of the programs and activities are not truly building the kingdom of God. They may be building our own local kingdoms, but not HIS kingdom. The only sacred cow in any church should be soul-winning and if what we are doing in the church is not truly producing souls, even if it is an evangelistic program, we need to look at it and decide whether it is worth doing. Sacred cows make good hamburger.

When I think about Jesus' ministry, I think about those on the outside of the kingdom and even on the outside of society. Jesus took His disciples with Him and showed them what ministry was about. He walked the streets. He was not trying to build a building or even raise money. He found people like the woman at the well who had been married five times and was 'shacking up', the woman caught in adultery, the demoniac in the tombs, the blind beggar Bartimaeus, the ten lepers who no one wanted to touch and the tax-collectors. Then he showed them how valuable they were and blessed them, helped them and healed them.

When the lost, sick, poor, homeless, and brokenhearted come to our church, they should feel very welcome. There should be no 'clutter' or stumbling-blocks that keep them from finding the love, mercy and power of God. Jesus should be the only stumbling-block in our churches. Often, it is the other religious trappings that turn people off. It is the show, the professionalism, the swift-judgment, and the emphasis on religious success. People today are not resistant to Jesus---they are resistant to the people of God. Jesus was asked, "…Lord, when did we see You hungry, and feed You, or thirsty, and give You drink? And when did we see You a stranger, and invite you in, or naked, and clothe you? And when did we see You sick, or in prison, and come to You?" and Jesus answered, "…Truly, I say to you, to the extent that you did it to one of these brothers of Mine, even the least of them, you did it to Me." (Matthew 25:37-40)

WITHOUT WALLS

Because of where our church was and who we were reaching out to, this became our default ministry. We did not have a core group to start with. This may have helped us to actually become embedded in the community. The poor ones we reached became the leaders and core group. Even though I did not know what I was doing (and still don't according to some), God blessed us with 'walking testimonies'. Then he began to ask me to consider multiplying by training them how to disciple others.

It was during this time that we were trying to open the men's house. We were also struggling with the people selling the buildings we were renting. During the whole process of potentially losing our building, I went through battles with discouragement. On a Sunday night, I was returning home from church and I looked up into the sky. It was the most beautiful array of stars I had seen in a long time. I stared up at the wondrous beauty of God's creation and began to praise Him. After pondering the greatness of God, I asked God if I could see a shooting star. "Please send me a shooting star," I said. God said, "Why do you want to see a shooting star?" I said, "So I know You love me and are with me in this difficult time." He said, "You already know that. It is written in My word." I said, "I just need a little assurance." He said, "A wicked generation asks for a sign." I said, "Oops! Okay, never mind." The next night I was coming in again from the car and I looked at the beautiful night sky again. Again, I asked for a shooting star. Again, no answer.

Two nights later, I was at a meeting with some pastors. The speaker was talking and I felt he was purposely sharpshooting me. This hurt my feelings. He did, however, begin to speak of a church that did not need a building. A church that was on the streets and in homes. God said to me, "That's for you." I thought maybe God was not going to allow us to keep the buildings. When I came home, I was on the way in from the car with my head hanging down. All of a sudden, I saw a shooting star out of the corner of my eye. God said, "You did not really need to know I love you before. You did tonight and I promised to meet all of your needs." I was encouraged and then when I entered the house, the Lord led me to turn on TBN immediately. There was a man on Bishop Eddie Long's show talking about a church without walls that met on the streets. God said, "That's for you!" The next morning, a pastor friend called me. He said, "Last night there was a man on Bishop Eddie Long's show and the Lord showed me that you saw it. It was about a church on the streets. I felt that was really a message for you." Again, I was amazed at the greatness of God!

I started a journey of prayer for the ministry. God began to show me that it involved bringing good news *and* groceries to the streets. He also showed me that it involved churches working together, and Bible studies on the streets.

When we began Without Walls Ministry, I knew we needed vehicles. In January, the church began to pray. A Church of God called us out of the blue and donated a fifteen-passenger van. A Presbyterian church called us and gave us another. Then a man from Myrtle Beach called and gave us a pickup truck. Another friend called and gave us a pickup truck. A plumber called and gave us a cargo van. A church called and gave us two buses. A lady from the church bought a bus over the internet. Without even making our need known, the Lord provided us with three buses, four vans and two pickup trucks!

We had our first WOW (WithOut Walls) outreach and 20 people showed up which is the exact number we prayed for. I spent a lot of my time on my way back from picking up a bus from Kentucky praying for a CPA to work with the church. Almost immediately as I arrived into town, Brian Kurtz called me and said that he was starting a CPA firm and wanted to know if our church needed help. He began to tithe time to the church by coming in for four hours a week.

We had prayed for three buses for the church. First, Rhonda Arrington bought a bus over the internet without even asking us. I thought she wanted us to pay her for it, but she did not. Then, as I was at District Council, God led me to ask Pastor Lewis Gunn from Lake Wylie Christian Assembly about a bus. He mentioned that Christian Life Assembly (where we were) was trying to sell two buses. Tommy Reeves, a pastor at the church walked by right then and I stopped him and I asked him about it. He said that just that week they decided to give the buses to ministries. He said they would give us one, but they ended up giving us two!

We were on our way to a "Without Walls" Ministry.

CHAPTER 7

PHILOSOPHY OF WITHOUT WALLS

I was part of a church that had a great evangelistic program. It was great in that we were consistently going out into the community and sharing the gospel---making the claims of Scripture clear pertaining to eternal life. We trained a lot of people and that was good, but in the three years I was involved in it, I do not remember one new person who actually was saved, that was discipled and grafted into the church. I thought that this was the whole point and it was disillusioning that we are not seeing that kind of fruit.

God had done so much to help me in my life and I desperately wanted others to know. I was searching for the ministry He had for me to win souls. There are many methods of evangelism out there. We can hand out bottled water with our church's name on it. We can go door-to-door. We can hold an evangelistic crusade or hand out tracts. I have been involved in many of these activities and churches all over are doing them. Our problem is that while some churches are gaining numbers, the church in the United States is losing ground. Therefore, the growth that we are seeing in certain churches may not be Kingdom-growth but rather transfer-growth from one church to another.

SMALLER IS BETTER

I believe one of the reasons we are not seeing as much conversion growth in the church is the 'professionalism' in the ministry. There is much focus on excellence in what we are doing. There is so much focus on that, that many average people look at what church leaders do and think they could not do it. I heard a man teaching once. He asked his class to go to a large church with over a thousand attendees and watch the people ministering. He asked the class if they thought they could pastor that church or do what the staff was doing in ministry. They all responded with a resounding "No!" Then he asked them to visit a church with an attendance of about 75. When asked whether the class could accomplish what the staff was doing in that particular church, they all responded with "Yes" or "Maybe". He then made the point that the smaller church was more of a threat to the devil than the other because people could envision themselves ministering in that environment.

I wonder if Peter could have pastored a mega-church. Can you picture James and John in designer suits in big offices overlooking the city? Jesus himself was a carpenter and not a professional. He was a blue-collar worker and not a clergy-man with a graduate degree. He spent his time investing his life in a few willing followers. He never built a building, never raised over a million dollars for a project, never had a capital campaign, and did not own a big home in the country. He did not own an Armani suit or, perhaps, even a gold ring. He simply was a loving, powerful, truthful, homeless carpenter. "...and we beheld His glory, glory as of the only begotten from the Father, full of grace and truth." (John 1:14)

Interestingly enough, smaller churches are more effective

per capita in winning souls. "As numbers pass the one thousand mark, church health is increasingly difficult to maintain…"[7] A higher percentage of people are involved in ministry in a smaller church as well. In addition, it costs less per capita to keep a small church going. In virtually all measures of true productivity, effectiveness and fruitfulness, smaller churches win. Even though this is true, we are still drawn to the larger churches as examples. I remember going to a conference once about how to break the '200 barrier' (200 in attendance). My question, at that time, was how to break the '50 barrier'. I was constantly trying to learn from the pastors of these huge churches who had a totally different scenario than I did. The principles they were using did not fit my situation and that made me feel devalued.

As I look back, I now think that often as human beings we lift up things that are large and noticeable, but we forget the simple things that are productive. Consider Jesus noticing the widow giving her two copper coins. In the eyes of God she was giving more than the Pharisees who were sounding their trumpets. She was giving everything she had. Percentage-wise, she was a far more generous giver. I almost feel this is the way we are approaching ministry today. We lift up the large and noticeable ministries but we may be missing out on the ministries that are, per-capita, more effective and are really doing the work. We focus on growing larger and larger ministries and forget the importance of the multiplication of smaller churches.

For instance, there is an emphasis on 'excellence in ministry' in local churches today. I am certainly not against excellence, but I believe it is emphasized more than what the Bible calls for. "Today's overemphasis on the pursuit of excellence has led to a highly competitive attitude among churches and church leaders that's not matched in recent history."[8] We have idolized our performance and business-mindedness to the detriment of our soul-winning. I wonder if the church at Philippi that met down by the river had a 'commitment to excellence'. I wonder how many hours their worship team practiced so that their music was impeccable and perhaps the people from First Church of Ephesus might hear about their sound quality and want to check it out. Well, doesn't having our act together contribute to soul-winning? Maybe, but I think the stats tell us we are far off from being the soul-saving stations we are supposed to be.

I noticed once at a 'missions' banquet that awards were given to the highest overall giving churches. Everyone already knew who they would be. Sometimes, one would be more than the other, but it was always the same churches. No one thought to recognize per-capita giving, which was what Jesus recognized.

I wondered often why in three years of King's Kidz ministry in the projects on Saturdays with our 30 kids or so, it never rained. We tried to be excellent, but with only about four workers who were former alcoholics or schizophrenics, it was not easy. We did have a heart though. It was tough. Then, the drug dealers would threaten us or bother us or try to hinder the children from coming to the meetings. It really only rained once while I was out of town. A couple had agreed to lead but I did not realize they were living together and not married. I believe God did not want them infecting those kids with their ungodly lifestyle. Holiness is important in God's church.

ACCOUNTABILITY

I have noticed that accountability is easier with a smaller church. The hard-core discipline and accountability that was necessary to encourage change and healing in the lives of those who were sent to us when we first started were only possible in a smaller setting. I believe this could be possible in a larger setting but only with tremendous accountability through the leaders of the smaller groups. Someone would have to be truly inspecting, encouraging, exhorting and correcting the leaders.

Unfortunately, there is little accountability in the church today. God says that righteousness exalts a nation. The church is dying in America today partly, I believe, because the people in the church are no different than those outside. One of the reasons for this is that there is little expectation and follow-through from church leaders when it comes to holy living of church members. With our current performance-based church mentality, church becomes, perhaps, more of a 'show' than what God wants. We need to find a way to express and encourage Godly expectations for church members.

MINISTRY TO THE POOR

As I have already mentioned before, I believe one of the biggest oversights in my Christian life, for the first six years, was ministry to the poor. I read the Bible and was involved in church. I felt I was following God and had a great sense of satisfaction in my relationship with Him. I was productive in discipling those whom He sent my way. Somehow, even though I read my Bible through every year, I somehow missed the call to reach the poor. I missed the call to visit those in prison. I missed the widows and orphans. I do not know how, but I missed it.

It is so important that we make a priority of serving the poor. It is the outworking of our faith and an evidence of our faith that we serve the poor. The Bible says that if we see a brother in need of food and clothing and do nothing to help, but tell them to be warmed and fed, that is the same as faith without works. As a matter of fact, "There are nearly 400 biblical passages demonstrating God's concern for the orphans, widows, prisoners, aliens, the homeless, the poor, the hungry, the sick, and the disabled…."[9] "(Josiah)… pled the cause of the afflicted and needy; then it went well with him. Is not that what it means to know me?" (Jeremiah 22:15b–16) When Paul was commissioned as a minister of the gospel, the one warning he was given that is recorded in Scripture was to "remember the poor". (Galatians 2:10) Also"…let us do good to all men…" (Galatians 6:10) Virtually all of the books of the Bible equate relieving the needs of the poor with righteousness.

Consider that Aristedes, a Christian apologist in first century Athens describing Christians to the Roman Emporer Hadrian, "They love one another. They never fail to help widows; they save orphans from those who would hurt them. If they have something, they give freely to the man who has nothing. If they see a stranger, they take him home, and are happy, as though he were a real brother." I believe this partially reflects Jesus' vision for the church. If the church in America would rise up, we could offer our country the system of support people are looking for in the welfare system. "…the homeless, incarcerated, widows, orphans, and immigrants generally lack a social support system. As the largest social support system in the United States, the church has the potential to greatly expand the kingdom by providing social support for those who have none." (Michael Elliott,

President, Union Mission in Savannah, Georgia) The church offers community to those who have no community. God "sets the lonely in families." (Psalm 68:6)

Consider this: "Good deeds and good news cannot and should not be separated...Patrick was the first public man to speak out against slavery... The Irish slave trade came to a halt, and other forms of violence such as murder and intertribal warfare decreased, and his communities modeled the Christian way of faithfulness, generosity and peace to all the Irish."[10] Christians should be known as the ones who do good and stand up for the oppressed. We are the salt of the earth and the light of the world.

DISCIPLESHIP

"Salt, light and leaven do not work very well at a distance."[11]

Jesus' Great Commission was for us to go into all the world and make disciples. When we first started our church in the inner-city, this was a priority. We did not have any members, let alone leaders, so our goal became to raise up leaders from the community. This involved intensive involvement in their lives, watching the Holy Spirit take charge as they surrendered to God and began to understand how to apply it to their lives. It was truly amazing to watch lives transform before our eyes.

Andy Stanley, pastor and writer, asked, "How do you know a church is winning?"[12] He gives a possible answer as relevant teaching and changed lives. If your ministry is not seeing lives changed, then you need to change. He says, "If the win is unclear, you may force those in leadership roles to define winning in their own terms."[13]

As we developed, keeping up the programs became too

much of a priority. We have been trying to start more and more things and keep them going. All 'good' ideas and programs are not 'God' ideas and programs. *He wants to bring us back to simplicity and the basics.* Programs that take up tremendous amounts of time and money, but do not truly produce new converts and successful discipleship, contributes to clutter the ministry and steal precious resources away from what is most important.

Imagine if most of our time in religious activity was spent in person-to-person discipleship and developing people---particularly reaching and teaching the lost, poor and brokenhearted. What if the time we spent in developing programs was spent ministering one-on-one to those who simply needed someone to show them the way and then they were released to do the same with others.

PEOPLE, NOT BUILDINGS

"In many cases, it is the property, more than the calling, mission, or opportunity, that dictates the form and amount of ministry a church provides."[14]

I have heard more than one pastor say that if you want to know a church that is going somewhere, look for the one that has a building project underway. Our affinity for buildings sometimes seems to outshine our affinity for lost souls. "Churches today have become land developers instead of people developers."[15] While homeless souls and the poor and brokenhearted are on the streets waiting for us to bring them the love of Jesus in Word and deed, we are excited about the latest new teaching or experience we can have with God.

OUTSIDE THE WALLS

Jesus told us to follow Him and that He would make us fishers of men. What would it mean to follow Jesus into His ministry? Would it mean a professional staff, huge buildings that sit empty 90% of the time, large choirs and bands, and ski trips? God may not be against these things, but *the style of ministry exhibited by Jesus had a different emphasis.*

As we ponder Jesus' style of ministry, I think we will note that the majority of it took place on the streets and hillsides instead of in the temples and cathedrals. Jesus knew that was where we would find the lost and hurting. Many of the lost do not even feel comfortable in our church buildings. They do not understand what we are doing and the love of Jesus. It is up to us to go to them and demonstrate His love where they are.

Miracles often happened on the streets. As part of our outreach, we would visit the same people every week and ask them if there was anything that we could do to serve them. Please recall the man we visited for a year and a half mentioned in Chapter 5. After receiving a refrigerator through our ministry and prayer for his drinking problem when he lost his job, he joined our men's house. After six months in the men's house, I asked him what God had been teaching him. He said God was showing him that he answers prayer. He reminded me about the refrigerator. Then he reminded me that he and I had prayed for a guitar for him and within a week someone brought one by the church as a donation. Then he prayed for an amp and someone gave him one. Then one night at all-night prayer, he asked for us to pray for healing for his chronic back pain. When we prayed, it was gone. It had been hurting for years but God set him free! He is a living miracle for Jesus today.

One thing we discovered at Without Walls Ministry, an outreach ministry uniting churches to reach outside the four walls, was that our prayers did not just affect individuals and our ministry, but also the neighborhoods we were in. Sometimes we would simply walk the neighborhood and pray. We would come up with a prayer list and a vision for the neighborhood we were in and then pray specifically for the vision to come to pass.

One weekend I went to Without Walls. A common prayer request for the apartment complex was security, the doors staying locked, and for an alarm system. God told me to walk around the inside of the complex three times and pray for this and for His angelic protection---for divine protection. That Sunday, I went to the complex to pick people up for church. Interestingly, I went to open one of the doors that had been broken for over a year. When I pulled on it, it was locked! God reminded me about our little walk. Clayton went to a meeting for me at the apartment complex to deliver chairs. At the meeting was a man from ADT who spoke about how they were coming in to secure the building! PRAISE GOD! Additionally, God asked me, months later, to pray for the salvation or removal of a woman who had been there for a long time, who was bringing a lot of confusion, drugs, violence and problems into the complex. Within a month she was gone. It is so much more peaceful there now!

We are like UPS (United People in Service). We are not here to warehouse people. We are here to package them up and send them out.

UNITY

God reminded us that where His people dwell in unity, God will command a blessing. "Behold, how good and how pleasant it is for brothers to dwell together in unity! It is like the precious oil upon the head, coming down upon the beard, even Aaron's beard, coming down upon the edge of his robes. It is like the dew of Hermon, coming down upon the mountains of Zion; For there the LORD commanded the blessing---life forever." (Psalm 133) I believe unity will also be a factor that welcomes the Holy Spirit's anointing in the next great revival. The disciples were all in one accord when the Spirit came. Ephesians 4:13 indicates that as the church matures and prepares for Christ's coming, it must become more united.

Without Walls ministry has seen some wonderful miracles, I think partly because of unity. As each church adopts its own neighborhoods, there can be a cooperation to win a whole city. My father-in-law has a pond he allows the family members and friends to fish in. I have been fishing with 4 or 5 other people and we may have caught 10 or 20 fish. One year, my father-in-law decided to 'draw' the pond. Many family members gathered together and he let most of the water out of the pond. We all grabbed part of a very long net and worked our way across the pond. Each of us had our own area of the net to make sure the fish did not slip through. The result was a harvest of hundreds of fish. This reflects the power of working together and uniting in the harvest.

Imagine a city where each church adopts neighborhoods. They go out and meet needs and build relationships on a weekly basis. They build relationships by visiting the same people every week, just showing love with no strings attached. They offer people rides from those neighborhoods to their services. They start Bible studies in the neighborhoods. The gospel is preached on the streets and hillsides and in homes. Each church is handing out food and helping people with service-projects in their neighborhoods.

Imagine those churches working together to establish a ministry-center where there are resources of food, tools, vehicles, sound systems and more that each church can use. The churches gather together to praise and worship on a regular basis. United prayer goes up for the city. They occasionally bring people from the neighborhoods to large scale parties where the poor and brokenhearted are brought from the highways and byways to join together and celebrate the Savior.

This sort of ministry would facilitate unity, prayer, effective evangelism, care for the needy, accountability, and love. I believe large fishing nets could be spread over entire cities with the love of Jesus---and revival could be the outcome.

Imagine a city, on the other hand, where churches are constantly asking people to come to them. Imagine that the churches are competing with their programs and doing everything they can to fill up their buildings, sometimes at the expense of other churches. Imagine a competitive spirit among the churches. The churches do not have poor people in them. The homeless people do not go to the churches.

I believe the choice is ours. I know most Christian leaders and church members want to unite. They want to reach the poor. They want to effectively win the lost. If what we are doing now is not working, I know God must have a better way. He said He would build His church and the gates of Hell would not prevail against it. Let us continue to pray and work unto that end!

ENDNOTES

1. Brown, Stephen R. "America, the New Mission Field", First Assembly of God, Charleston, SC, October, 2009 (Powerpoint presentation)

2. Fraser, Walter J., Jr. *Charleston! Charleston!*, Columbia, SC: University of South Carolina Press, 1989.

3. Brown, Stephen R. "America, the New Mission Field", First Assembly of God, Charleston, SC, October, 2009 (Powerpoint presentation)

4. Kendall, R.T. *Total Forgiveness*, Lake Mary, Fl: Charisma House Publishers, 2002.

5. Rusaw, Rick & Eric Swanson, *The Externally Focused Church*, Loveland, CO: Group Publishing, 2004, pg. 115

6. Stevens, Selwyn, "Freemasonry", St. John's Episcopal Church, March, 2010. (Lecture)

7. Sjogren, Steve. *The Perfectly Imperfect Church*, Loveland, CO: Group Publishing, 2002, pg. 16

8. Sjogren, Steve. *The Perfectly Imperfect Church*, Loveland, CO: Group Publishing, 2002, pg. 18

9. Rusaw, Rick & Eric Swanson, *The Externally Focused Church*, Loveland, CO: Group Publishing, 2004, pg. 18

10. Rusaw, Rick & Eric Swanson, *The Externally Focused Church*, Loveland, CO: Group Publishing, 2004, pg. 24

11. Rusaw, Rick & Eric Swanson, *The Externally Focused Church*, Loveland, CO: Group Publishing, 2004, pg. 25

12. Stanley, Andy, Reggie Joiner & Lane Jones, *Seven Practices of Effective Ministry*, Sisters, Oregon: Multnomah Press, 2004, pg. 7

13. Stanley, Andy, Reggie Joiner & Lane Jones, *Seven Practices of Effective Ministry*, Sisters, Oregon: Multnomah Press, 2004, pg.73

14. Easum, Bill, *Beyond the Box*, Loveland, CO: Group Publishing, 2003, pg.13

15. Easum, Bill, *Beyond the Box*, Loveland, CO: Group Publishing, 2003, pg.124

CPSIA information can be obtained at www.ICGtesting.com
Printed in the USA
LVOW061231191211

260126LV00001B/1/P